Please return/renew this item by the last date shown.

To renew this item, call **0845 0020777** (automated)
or visit **www.librarieswest.org.uk**

Borrower number and PIN required.

Libraries**West**

D0419939

Derek Hill

CHARLIE KAUFMAN AND HOLLYWOOD'S MERRY BAND OF PRANKSTERS, FABULISTS AND DREAMERS: AN EXCURSION INTO THE AMERICAN NEW WAVE

kamera
BOOKS

First published in 2008 by Kamera Books
PO Box 394, Harpenden, Herts, AL5 1XJ
www.kamerabooks.com

Copyright © Derek Hill, 2008
Series Editor: Hannah Patterson

A CIP catalogue record for this book is available from the British Library.

ISBN-13: 978-1-84243-253-2

Typeset by Elsa Mathern
Printed by CPI Cox & Wyman, Reading, RG1 8EX

Dedicated to Lynda, my partner in mischievousness. This book could not have been possible without her invaluable insight, patience and, most importantly, her support.

ACKNOWLEDGEMENTS

I would like to thank my editor Hannah Patterson for the opportunity to write this and for her patience with me. Joe Pettit, Jr. for his help with research materials and support, Lisa Moore for her friendship and words of wisdom over the years, Shawn Levy for his encouragement and help, Joe Kane at *VideoScope*, Jackie Acampora at *Mystery Scene*, Todd Grimson, and Michelle... just because.

I also want to thank my mom, who rarely showed parental guidance when it came to my movie watching at an impressionable age. I am grateful. She unknowingly set me loose to explore all that is sublime and wretched. No doubt she would be shocked by some of my choices, but I hope she is pleased with the outcome of it all.

CONTENTS

INTRODUCTION

An American No Wave

We've been here before. Film movements are nothing new, though sadly they seem like a rarity nowadays. It's as if the idea of a group of filmmakers intentionally attempting to spark a revolution with their cameras is too dated, too romantic and too ridiculous even to ponder. It appeals to the ambitious 14-year-old within, even though the older, wiser, more cynical adult knows better.

But there is no reason why the genuine, conscious, aesthetic movement – with or without manifesto – determined to subvert the mainstream culture at large with its transcendental images should necessarily be a thing of the past. The history of film comprises such movements, whether they are of a philosophical nature or simply a stylistic one – even when not all members were *conscious* of being part of the respective movement, such as the workmanlike visionaries behind the films noirs. The 1940s had Italian Neo-Realism. The 1950s had the British Kitchen Sink dramas. The 1960s had the French *nouvelle vague* (which subsequently spawned new waves across Europe in Italy, Czechoslovakia, Poland, Hungary, Korea, and Japan). The 1970s had the New German Cinema. And most recently there has been the rabble-rousing Dogma 95 bunch. Issuing a manifesto to the world in 1995, this filmmaker collective, which included Lars Von Trier and Thomas Vinterberg among its founding members, declared a 'rescue action' upon films that perpetuated the Hollywood myth of gimmickry, illusion, and lies. Brandishing a system of rules known as the 'Vows of Chastity', the Dogma 95 clan individually waged a cleansing campaign against artifice, mandating that 'shooting must be done on location'; 'sound must never be produced apart from the images or vice versa'; 'the film must not take place where the camera is standing'; 'shooting must take place where the film takes place'; 'the film must be in colour'; 'genre movies are not acceptable', and so on. Directors who did not submit to these tenets were publicly reprimanded. Filmmakers who did adhere received a certificate and the guiltless sleep of a job well done.

Contentious, over-the-top, deadly humorous, and equally serious-minded, what started out as four films – Vinterberg's *Festen/The Celebration* (1998), Von Trier's *Idioterne/The Idiots* (1998), Søren Kragh-Jacobson's *Mifunes Sidste Sang/Mifune* (1999) and Kristian Levering's *The King is Alive* (2000) – eventually grew to over 200, though the originators of this conscious movement soon abandoned the stringencies of their own rules when it became increasingly clear that Dogma 95 was becoming a genre all its own – a notion that was anathema to what was originally intended.

Recently in American cinema there have been furtive whispers (appropriately enough) about a so-called mumblecore aka bedhead cinema.[1] With minuscule budgets, non-pro casts and determined filmmakers such as Andrew Bujalski, Aaron Katz, Joe Swanberg, and the Duplass Brothers keeping their modest films low to the ground, the DIY spirit of filmmaking seems to be alive and if not well... well then, awake. Focused on predominantly urban, middle-class, white college kids and their problems with relationships, and the intransigent nature of life in their 20s, this post-millennial, mostly digital video-lensed (though Bujalski does shoot on celluloid) MySpace cinema, at its best, accurately chronicles the lives of its hazy-headed protagonists. But at its worst, this more-Henry-Jaglom-than-John-Cassavetes movement seems nothing more than American independent cinema at its most conservative, regressive, provincial, and imaginatively stagnant. Only time will determine the overall importance of directors such as Bujalski, Katz, and Swanberg. But while the lasting impact of the mumblecore films is still up for debate, there's no arguing that these truly independent filmmakers (many of the films don't even get shown at the Sundance Film Festival) are a refreshing alternative to many of the pseudo-indies subsidised by the major studios which flood Sundance every year.

Rumours abound that a cabal of American filmmakers, known not-so-secretly as the 'Pizza Knights', gather once a month to watch and study American films of the 1970s, the so-called New Hollywood era or age of the Movie Brats.[2] But considering the disparate array of filmmakers who supposedly attend these periodic events – Wes Anderson, David Fincher, Spike Jonze, Steven Soderbergh, Roman Coppola, Alexander Payne, Kimberly Peirce, among others – and taking into account their own varied cinematic contributions, the secret order of the Pizza Knights seems more like a clubhouse of industry insiders who just dig good movies and want to hang out than a definable, significant movement.

Then where does that leave us? Has there been no real American film movement since the days when Coppola, Scorsese, Altman, Ashby, Cassavetes, Mazursky, Spielberg, and Lucas, among others, stormed the gates of the Hollywood establishment and, for a brief moment, took over and ushered in an aesthetic renaissance? Even then, though, the advent of the New Hollywood was an unconscious 'movement' based on purely commercial grounds – the box-office success of *Easy Rider* (1969) – that eventually opened the doorway to more substantial artistic opportunities. Did the flame of overthrow really die out when the directors of the New Hollywood tempered their own rebellion? I don't think so, since the filmmakers discussed in this book commonly share stylistic and thematic characteristics that could well be viewed as a movement.

But before we jump to the present… a few words on the *nouvelle vague* and New Hollywood.

The Nouvelle Vague

The details that explain the emergence of the *nouvelle vague*, a term that journalist François Giroud originally coined in 1958 in *L'Express*, seem slightly ridiculous in retrospect, perhaps a bit too romantic and contrived, as if they were all the recollections of an aging sentimental dreamer. But we have the writings, the interviews and, of course, the films to prove the dreamer correct. And though, as famously stated in John Ford's 1962 film, *The Man Who Shot Liberty Valance*, it's always preferable to print the legend over the facts, in this case the facts are as alluring as the legend.

Like their literary American counterparts the Beats (Kerouac, Ginsberg, Burroughs), these Gallic hipster provocateurs were seeking something more tangible and meaningful to their lives beyond post-World War II prosperity, industrialisation and bourgeois comfort and complacency. Out of the wreckage of that war's aftermath, the seeds of a burgeoning film movement were germinating. With little money and no real hands-on experience (though plenty of experience and know-how gleaned from watching innumerable films), these ambitious art criminals stormed the cinema houses across the globe and proclaimed a crusade against the glossy, formal and, in essence, dead mainstream films that were the backbone of the French movie industry at the time. The *nouvelle vague* filmmakers were cinema literate, intelligent and shrewd, and their films were unlike anything that the world had seen. It was life projected, preserved, and volatile like the cinema hadn't experienced in years.

The main culprits in the subsequent and short-lived overthrow – François Truffaut, Jean-Luc Godard, Claude Chabrol, Jacques Rivette, and Eric Rohmer – were a group of passionate, militant young men who religiously gathered at the cathedral of cinema in Paris, the Cinémathèque Française, to gobble up the images of the world at 24 frames per second and passionately argue the merits (or lack thereof) of whatever the Cinémathèque's co-founder and de facto archivist, preservationist, and saviour Henri Langlois served up. As cineastes, Truffaut, Godard, et al devoured films from all over the world, sans subtitles, and gained their formative film education within the smoky twilight world of the *Cinémathèque* before making their own creative imprints upon reality.

While at the cultural epicentre of celluloid, the *Cinémathèque* was not the only catalyst for these soon-to-be-world-class filmmakers to make films themselves. Truffaut, Godard, Chabrol, Rivette, and Rohmer all wrote for the influential *Cahiers du cinéma* journal. Within its pages the group dissected and carved out their theory of the *politique des auteurs*, a theory that was simple enough in concept – that the director was the dominant voice of his creation and that the astute cineaste could extract meaning from looking at a director's entire body of work to see a unified vision – but dramatically controversial and argued over by fellow critics and audiences throughout the world. And if the *Cahiers* bunch were to solidify the director as the sole 'voice' of his work, then they also had to decipher the various film genres, e.g. horror, film noir, crime films, westerns, or musicals, that the director was working in and how they maintained their voice. Brutally opinionated, Truffaut, Godard, and company began to systematise and form their critical designs under the guidance and protectiveness of the great theoretician and co-founder/editor of *Cahiers du cinéma*, André Bazin. Truffaut, more so than any of the others, subsequently owed many of his ideas about the shape of films to come to Bazin.

Undoubtedly the most important critic and theorist in the post-World War II years, Bazin's early writings were published in numerous magazines, journals and reviews before he embarked on co-founding *Cahiers* in 1951. The journal, along with its rival *Positif* (formed a year after *Cahiers du cinéma*), championed American cinema from the 1950s and was stridently focused on engaging the serious-minded cineaste in seeking out the miraculous within the images before them… if the film, of course, was worthy of carrying such wonders.

Their approach to viewing film was liberating. The prize was not necessarily in being able to perfectly evaluate a film as a whole but to lose oneself in the moment, to fall under the spell of the image. It was a quest for the real: to find profundity within the mundane. For the *nouvelle vague* directors, their films were a plea for reality within the construct of an artificial medium, just as painters, writers, composers, and poets had similarly yearned before them. Despite their revolutionary approaches and end results, the concept of capturing 'reality' was nothing new. Before Truffaut and Godard ever hefted a camera upon their slight shoulders, the Italian Neo-Realists of the late 1940s had attempted much the same – to capture life in the moment.

The *Cahiers du cinéma* critics, who were more catholic and conservative in their theory of the auteur than the *Positif* gang, believed that the generation of filmmakers before them, with very few exceptions, were failures because they refused to dig deep, loosen up and document life in the present even at the risk of 'destroying' the reality of the illusion. They were disgusted with the absence of a distinctive director's personality, which subsequently meant that there was an absence of a direct relationship with the audience. Much of the *Cahiers* critics' antipathy was directed toward the popular French cinema at the time, what Truffaut labelled the 'quality tradition' of stage-bound melodramas, costume dramas and generally respectable, impersonal cinema. These were the slick mainstream, literary-based, financially successful films of the time. Ironically enough, it would be the financial success of the 'quality tradition' productions that eventually made it possible for the upstarts of the *nouvelle vague* to make their own lower-budgeted, on-the-fly pictures. The advent of lighter, less expensive equipment was also an important boon.

Despite their lashing of the 'quality tradition' films, a number of important French directors were not subjected to scorn. Directors like Jean Renoir, Jacques Becker, Jean-Pierre Melville, Jacques Tati, Robert Bresson, Agnès Varda, Louis Malle, and even Roger Vadim, who was closer in age to the *nouvelle vague* but already making studio films, were left unscathed. Varda and Malle were eventually swept up in the wave themselves.

Modernity gleefully crashed the stodgy party in 1959 when the first films by Chabrol and Truffaut were released. Although Truffaut's *Les Quatre cents coups/The 400 Blows* and Alain Resnais' *Hiroshima, mon amour* are frequently, *mistakenly*, given credit for being the first *nouvelle vague* films, Claude Chabrol's films *Le Beau Serge/Handsome Serge* and *Les Cousins* were released a year earlier to critical acclaim but far less impact. Regardless of the chronology of events, Resnais and Truffaut's films would become landmarks of the *nouvelle vague*, setting the stage for an onslaught of classic, unforgettable films. Truffaut's partially autobiographical debut would become a monumental success the world over, eventually winning the young director the Grand Prize at the Cannes Film Festival in 1959. By the time that Truffaut released his second film, *Tirez sur le pianiste/Shoot the Piano Player*, a year later, critics and audiences would not be so kind.

Over the next couple of years, Rohmer, Rivette, and Godard – the latter with his bubble-gum explosion *À bout de souffle/Breathless* (1959) – added their own disparate contributions to the aesthetic onslaught against complacency. But the *nouvelle vague* was never just about theory or militant aesthetics. Style, and the ability to pull off a more free-and-easy, almost improvisatory atmosphere, was mostly due to their budgetary constraints and the access to inexpensive, lighter cameras and equipment. Even today the look and feel of the primary films is ecstatic, energising, and inventive. The great Raoul Coutard, the 'midwife of the *nouvelle vague*'[3], filmed most of them. His influence, one of lasting art and functionality, can be felt and seen in the work of Lance Acord, the cinematographer and frequent collaborator of many of the filmmakers discussed in this book. On a purely technical level, the influence of Coutard – who worked primarily with Truffaut and Godard – upon filmmaking has been immeasurable; and his work has been rightfully praised for its simplicity, beauty, and his ability as a keen improviser, especially in his collaborations with Godard. The images that Coutard created with his directors – Jean-Paul Belmondo and Jean Seberg strolling down the streets of Paris or lounging in bed, a cigarette perpetually lazing from Belmondo's lips in Godard's *À bout de souffle*; Anna Karina's tears in *Vivre sa vie/My Life to Live* (1962); the startling use of colour in both Godard's *Le Mépris/Contempt* (1963) and *Pierrot le fou* (1965) – are some of the most famous and memorable ever conceived in world cinema.

By the time many of the filmmakers were mounting or planning their second films, they were also looking for ways to challenge themselves further on technical and thematic grounds. Throughout the decade, the filmmakers of the *nouvelle vague* consistently decimated the traditional narrative form and film language. Whether it was the use of sudden jump cuts, use of ironic intertitles, long tracking shots, or working with non-actors with only the barest script, the *nouvelle vague* was always about capturing life as it really was even if it risked destroying the illusion. Ideas or expectations of what a film genre could be – e.g. the musical (as with Godard's *Une femme est une femme/A Woman is a Woman* from 1961 and Jacques Demy's 1964 film, *Les Parapluies de Cherbourg/The Umbrellas of Cherbourg*), the crime film (*À bout de souffle*; *Tirez sur le pianiste*) or the historical romance (*Jules et Jim*) – were consistently turned inside out. In Godard's case, the utilisation of Brechtian distancing effects, calling attention to the distortion of the 'reality' being shown upon the screen (never more comically or obviously deployed than in his 1963 film *Les Carabiniers* in which a character attacks a movie screen after seeing his first images), was meant to heighten the illusion in a manner that would alienate the audience to the point where they would have to consciously think about what the images meant. But for all their revolutionary impact (and frequent posturing), the liberation was sometimes just plain aggravating, as many viewers no doubt felt with Godard's films in the late 1960s through the 1970s. In the end, though, the various methodologies, narrative instincts and cavalier style of the *nouvelle vague* was crucial evidence that a soul *can* exist at 24 frames per second.

By the late 1960s, the two brightest stars of the movement had taken very different paths. Truffaut, though successful and increasingly popular, mellowed a bit from his initial mercurial, uncompromising self, though he was still making fascinating films. Abandoning the wildly experimental and free-form inventiveness of his second film for a more classical and less distracting style, he would go on to make *Fahrenheit 451* (1965), based on the novel by Ray Bradbury and his first English-language production; *La Mariée était en noir/The Bride Wore Black* (1968) and *La Sirène du Mississippi/Mississippi Mermaid* (1969), both based on classic Cornell Woolrich noir novels; the historical film *Les Deux anglaises et le continent/Two English Girls* (1971); and *La Nuit américaine/Day for Night* (1973), his ode to the joys and humorous pitfalls of life on set, which would also earn him his first and only Academy Award for Best Foreign Language Film. Throughout his career, Truffaut also revisited his most famous and beloved character, Antoine Doinel from *Les Quatre cents coups*, in a number of films starring his cinematic double, Jean-Pierre Léaud. Sadly, Truffaut would die of a brain tumour in 1984, robbing us all of the cinematic possibilities to come.

Godard, on the other hand, ever the uncompromising militant intellectual, would stray from commercial filmmaking altogether after his blistering anti-capitalist, apocalyptic masterpiece, *Le Weekend/Week End* (1968). The film contains dizzying technical flourishes, from an extended tracking shot of a traffic jam to end all traffic jams along a rural highway, complete with burned-out cars and ravaged corpses, to footage of a hog being slaughtered on film – a powerful scene far more shocking than any of the mondo films that were fashionable at the time. The final intertitle that proclaimed 'Fin' then 'de Cinema' was an appropriate exit for a filmmaker who was growing more and more politicised. Godard would proclaim himself a revolutionary Maoist at this time and he eventually disengaged from the constraints of commercialism, rejecting all capitalist funding for his productions. His subsequent films were infused with radical Marxist ideas and equally radical ways of cinematically translating those ideas for the public. In 1972, though, he returned to a semblance of user-friendly cinema that was also one of his best, *Tout va bien*. Starring Jane Fonda and Yves Montand as a married couple (she as a reporter and he as a filmmaker who has 'sold out' his personal vision to make commercials) who get embroiled in a strike at a sausage factory, the film has many virtuosic moments, including the scenes of the stage-bound factory and a final long take within a horrendously commercialised supermarket where a riot eventually breaks out.

Despite the tendency to be undervalued and taken for granted by modern critics and audiences alike, the ever-troublesome Godard remains one of the true originals of the medium. Still working today, Godard managed to beguile and spark debate with the release of what many consider to be his crowning achievement, the 260-minute, surreal odyssey of the moving image entitled *Histoire(s) du Cinéma*. Made between 1988 and 1998 for French television, this sprawling, defiant and loving tribute to the Faustian image, shows that age has not tempered this always-challenging artist. And to remind the world that he was still as engaged with political struggle as ever, Godard released the controversial *Notre musique* in 2004, a semi-documentary structurally based on Dante's *Divine Comedy* focusing on war's insidious shadow over human lives, including a segment on the Israeli/Palestinian conflict.

The other main participants – Chabrol, Rivette, and Rohmer – likewise continued to make films. Chabrol eventually focused all of his attention on directing films in the crime genre, earning the appropriate label of the French Hitchcock. Simmering with understated menace, his films remain intelligent examinations of characters living with the darkest of hearts. Rivette, never known for his productivity, nevertheless continued to make personal films usually focused on the sometimes difficult relationships between artist and muse, like the four-hour *La Belle noiseuse* (1990). His most successful and haunting film, though, is his 1974 masterpiece, *Céline et Julie vont en bateau/Céline and Julie Go Boating*. Rohmer has continued making films as well. His subtle and exquisite examinations of male/female relationships in all of their psychological complexity – frequently organised under such headings as 'Six Moral Tales', 'Comedies and Proverbs' or 'Tales of the Four Seasons' – are primary examples of a more literary approach to film and character while ceasing to abandon the cinematic possibilities available.

Forty years on, the imprint of the *nouvelle vague* is still gigantic. But the films are anything but daunting, even when they are at their most cerebral and combative. Joyfully anarchic, hip, moving, reckless and thoughtful, they represent a world of riches awaiting the inquisitive yet cautious neophyte cineaste as well as the seasoned, jaded filmgoer, despite the best efforts of some critics to snuff out their wildness.

In 1959, a riot took place across cinema screens the world over. It's never really ended. You just have to know how to look.

The Movie Brats: Hollywood Regeneration

In the late 1960s, a revolution of sorts occurred. Fresh out of film school, a group of ambitious, hipster barbarians stormed the gates of the major Hollywood studios, bent on overthrowing the aging and increasingly out-of-tune studio heads embedded within their castle keeps. But it wasn't just Hollywood that was feeling that the times were indeed a-changin'. The entire country was fracturing due to the Vietnam War, the civil rights struggles and the women's liberation movement. There was blood in the streets and men on the moon... but Hollywood remained clueless.

The major studios had been creaking along for years before the first artistic shot was fired. The slick wheels of production had slowed their churn after a series of major financial flops – most notably Joseph L. Mankiewicz's lumbering epic *Cleopatra* (1963), starring Elizabeth Taylor and Richard Burton – and the persistent threat of television lured people away from the theatres. Much like the years leading up to the emergence of the *nouvelle vague*, when the French studios were, with few exceptions (such as the films of Jean Renoir, Robert Bresson, and Jean-Pierre Melville), cranking out efficient, stylish but vapid studio product, the Hollywood studios were likewise in need of something real, something dynamic to rejuvenate the industry. And like the scene in France, hardly anyone in Hollywood actually saw the first blow hammering down.

Modern filmmakers Quentin Tarantino and Paul Thomas Anderson, and writers like Peter Biskind, whose aggressively gossipy tome *Easy Riders, Raging Bulls* chronicled the highs and lows of the New Hollywood era with an addictive (if wrongheaded) zeal, have fetishised the films and pop culture of the 1970s ad nauseam. The film and television industry has also torn into the cadaver, 're-imagining' and re-packaging many of the era's more questionable television programmes – *The*

Brady Bunch, Charlie's Angels, The Dukes of Hazzard, Starsky and Hutch – into blockbuster movies or back into other questionable sit-coms (*Happy Days* transmutated into *That '70s Show*) for a whole new generation. Nevertheless, it's easy to get carried away with the myth of the times, pining for a return of the reckless auteur-with-final-cut who would risk everything for Art while sticking it to 'The Man', especially when one starts to roll out the names of the main super-star creative minds behind the camera (Francis Ford Coppola, Martin Scorsese, Robert Altman, Robert Towne, Brian De Palma, Paul Schrader, Steven Spielberg) and the stars (Jack Nicholson, Warren Beatty, Robert De Niro, Al Pacino, Dustin Hoffman) of the era. Emerging out of the detritus of pre-1967 Hollywood, these soaring talents with one foot in Europe and the other on Haight-Asbury managed for a while to convince the studios that there was loads of cash to be made from the exploding youth movement and that mainstream audiences might actually want to come along for the trip as well.

Like most revolutions, it began with a bang. *Bonnie and Clyde* was released in the summer of 1967, and the studio chiefs at Warner Bros were not exactly happy with star Warren Beatty and director Arthur Penn's sexy and rabidly violent film about real-life Depression-era gangsters Clyde Barrow and Bonnie Parker. Which was ironic consid-ering that the studio in the 1930s and early 1940s had made a fine art and profit out of bullets, blood, and bruisers with films such as *The Public Enemy* (1931), *G-Men* (1935), *Angels with Dirty Faces* (1938), and *The Roaring Twenties* (1939), all starring James Cagney, and *High Sierra* (1941), with Humphrey Bogart. As scripted by Hollywood new-comers David Newman and Robert Benton, the romanticised Bonnie and Clyde would become symbols of reckless youth, and the violence they unleashed would spark with the outrage of Vietnam-era America. And in contrast to the cinematic gangsters of the previous generation, who always had to pay for their crimes in the end or find redemp-tion due to Production Code advisements – or sometimes both (as in *Angels with Dirty Faces*) – these trigger-happy transgressors would remain defiantly unrepentant to the bloody end.

The Production Code of 1930 was a series of guidelines enforced by studio producers to curb 'immoral' behaviour in motion pictures, be it nudity or explicit renderings of sex and violence, fostering 'correct thinking' in the wild-eyed, fornicating, and violence-prone audiences. That was the theory, anyway. Tenets such as, 'No picture shall be produced that will lower the moral standards of those who see it. Hence the sympathy of the audience should never be thrown to the side of crime, wrongdoing, evil or sin, were for the most part obeyed right up into the late 1950s and early 1960s. By then, filmmakers such as Billy Wilder (with *Some Like it Hot* in 1959) and Alfred Hitchcock (with *Psycho* in 1960) were helping whittle away at the Code's strength by releasing films without approval. Mike Nichols' *Who's Afraid of Virginia Woolf?* (1966) and Michelangelo Antonioni's Swinging London existentialist thriller, *Blow-Up* (1966), deemed risky for their language and nudity respectively, also contributed to the dissolve of the antiquated guidelines.

But it was the revisionist *Bonnie and Clyde* that led the charge of unrest with the most vengeance. Taking its stylistic and emotional cues from the *nouvelle vague* instead of the gangster films of yore, the film jolted mainstream viewers out of their complacency with its potent cinematic death rattle of sexual frustration (Clyde's zeal for bloodshed is clearly linked to his impotence), ecstatic depictions of apocalyptic carnage and the cool bebop style of its fashionable anti-heroes. This was the moribund gangster as shape-shifted through the lens of the French film rebels while still maintaining a quintessentially American nonchalance and anti-intellectual vibe. Bonnie and Clyde's cinematic antecedents may have been Godard's beautiful losers – Belmondo and Seberg – but Beatty and Faye Dunaway would have never been allowed to have a dalliance with ideology (even the pose of one) like their Parisian compatriots. In Hollywood, where ideology usually amounted to a warm gun, style was always preferable to ideas.

Both Newman and Benton unhesitatingly acknowledged their love of Truffaut and Godard's films and the two Frenchmen were each approached in the early stages of development to possibly direct the film. The mind reels imagining what either one would have conjured up. Truffaut ultimately declined because of his commitment to *Fahrenheit 451*, while Godard reportedly became frustrated with the producers' inability to shoot fast and loose on location, a requirement as far as he was concerned.

But the *nouvelle vague* feel is ever-present. These Depression-era gangsters hurtled down the dusty backroads of East Texas with as much existential dread as their French counterparts, blissfully living a life of detours. They were hedonistic nihilists destined to destroy the new order, annihilate a world not ready to embrace change, freedom, and the right to look chic doing it. This was not your grandfather's gangster film by any means. This was 1967. This was the future.

After the mayhem wrought by *Bonnie and Clyde* (which was neither a critical nor financial success upon its initial release), a steady stream of vital films flowed into the movie houses echoing the turmoil and discontent beyond the cinema screen. *Easy Rider* (1969), the financial and cultural juggernaut that essentially broke down the Old Hollywood barrier once and for all, ushered in the era of New Hollywood behind its torched skidmarks. Regardless of it being nothing more than a hyper-psychedelic version of the youth-rebellion/biker-drive-in fare that Roger Corman had been turning out for years – like *The Wild Angels* (1966) – the film, which starred Peter Fonda, Jack Nicholson, and director Dennis Hopper, was a massive hit. The impact of Hopper's road-trip odyssey through the back roads of racist, oppressive, reactionary America was just the film to force Hollywood to take notice, if only for the clang of all those cash registers working overtime.

Over the next few years, the emergence of New Hollywood would take shape and solidify the overthrow of the old conservatism. Talented film-school brats (so-called because many of them, like Coppola, Scorsese, De Palma, George Lucas, Spielberg, John Milius, and John Carpenter were the first generation of film-school students to make inroads into the Hollywood establishment), rejuvenated Hollywood insiders (John Huston, Don Siegel, Robert Aldrich) and numerous others who either entered the fray after years toiling in television or were already earning their stripes working beneath the radar (Robert Altman,

Hal Ashby, Peter Bogdanovich, William Friedkin, Monte Hellman, Terrence Malick, Paul Mazursky, Sam Peckinpah, Bob Rafelson, to name just a few) would flood the marketplace with a variety of riches. This was the age of the film director as superstar, of newfound artistic freedom and ultimately incredible self-indulgence. But at its best, the range of quality productions released was remarkable – Altman's *McCabe & Mrs Miller* (1971), *The Long Goodbye* (1973), and *Nashville* (1975); Ashby's *The Last Detail* (1973) and *Shampoo* (1975); Coppola's *The Godfather* (1972), *The Godfather Part II* (1974), *The Conversation* (1974), and *Apocalypse Now* (1979); Bogdanovich's *The Last Picture Show* (1971); Friedkin's *The French Connection* (1971) and *The Exorcist* (1973); Sidney Lumet's *Dog Day Afternoon* (1975) and *Network* (1976); Malick's *Badlands* (1973) and *Days of Heaven* (1978); Peckinpah's *The Wild Bunch* (1969), *Straw Dogs* (1971), *Pat Garrett & Billy the Kid* (1973), and *Bring Me the Head of Alfredo Garcia* (1974); Roman Polanski's *Chinatown* (1974); Rafelson's *Five Easy Pieces* (1970) and *The King of Marvin Gardens* (1972); Mike Nichols' *The Graduate* (1967) and *Carnal Knowledge* (1971); and Scorsese's *Mean Streets* (1973), *Taxi Driver* (1976), and *Raging Bull* (1980), to name just some of the more notable titles, many of which are considered classics today.

But as with any film movement, especially one as broad and nebulous as New Hollywood, distortions and selective memory are the order of the day. The survivors of the mêlée (Altman, Coppola, Scorsese, Spielberg) have now crowded out directors who were once integral members (Richard Lester, Michael Ritchie, Hellman, Mazursky, Penn, Ashby) and many of the most vital and important films of the era – Lester's *Petulia* (1968), Robert Downey's *Putney Swope* (1969), Haskell Wexler's *Medium Cool* (1969), John Avildson's *Joe* (1970), Hellman's *Two-Lane Blacktop* (1971), Jerry Schatzberg's *Scarecrow* (1973), Penn's *Night Moves* (1975), Friedkin's *Sorcerer* (1977), Ulu Grosbard's *Straight Time* (1978) – have been relegated to the status of curiosities or footnotes, or forgotten altogether.

The end of New Hollywood was largely precipitated by the rise of the special-effects blockbuster, films like Spielberg's *Jaws* (1975) and

Lucas' *Star Wars* (1977) that paved the way for a new kind of manufactured designer movie hit, with less emphasis on character-driven storylines and more on spectacle. That was certainly not a new concept, but as Spielberg and Lucas ascended to become the new kings of the dream factory in the 1980s, the studios now flooded the theatres with a flurry of B-movie fantasy and science fiction productions with A-list big budgets. But it was director Michael Cimino's ill-fated, over-budget fiasco *Heaven's Gate* (1980), a lavishly produced political Western and follow-up to the Oscar-winning *The Deer Hunter* (1978), which is largely considered the death knell of New Hollywood. Not only did it ruin United Artists, its production studio, but it effectively dissolved the idea of a director's autonomy from the studio, with few exceptions. Financial flops, out-of-control productions and egomaniacal filmmakers are certainly not a thing of the past, but never again would a major studio allow a director to risk so many jobs and so much money to produce a few hours of entertainment.

The filmmakers of the New Hollywood did not die out. Some of them faded away, some died or became victims of their own private excesses, others were simply assimilated into the movie-making machine where they found greater success or scraped along, living and working within the shadows of their former greatness. But their collective legacy has continued to influence and dominate successive generations of young filmmakers spellbound by their work and they showed by example that it was possible for directors to make subversive, character-driven films within studio constraints.

And though the realities of an *auteur* working in Hollywood today are vastly different than they were in the 1970s, the filmmakers in this book – who all make films for the major studios – are proof that unique voices *can* still be heard within the wilderness… with a few broken hearts and bruises collected on the way, of course.

Charlie Kaufman: The Wizard of ID

'I really don't have any solutions and I don't like movies that do. I want to create situations that give people something to think about.

I hate a movie that will end by telling you that the first thing you should do is learn to love yourself. That is so insulting and condescending, and so meaningless. My characters don't learn to love each other or themselves.' – Charlie Kaufman[4]

What must have Charlie Kaufman been dreaming about while seated in the star-filled audience at the 2004 Academy Awards? Did he feel like a character in one of his own films – a bit dislocated though completely cognizant of their mental disintegration? Was he nervous, anxious and unable to remember the lines he'd written for himself in case he won? Did he feel his skin rub a little too closely against his bones, reminding him all too well that he was still a victim of his fears, insecurities and that ever-niggling bladder? Did he give in to mental revenge against all of the doubters, cynics and jackals that had surrounded him up to that moment, acknowledge the devil on his left just a bit more than the one on his right? Was he perhaps simply still in Malkovich's head? Or was he at home, so to speak, in front of the computer screen or the typewriter or the piece of paper that he always scribbled out a first draft on? Was he merely Charlie Kaufman from Massapequa, Long Island?

Kaufman won the Oscar that year, deservedly so, for *Eternal Sunshine of the Spotless Mind* (2004). When viewing footage of his acceptance speech, standing alongside his artistic collaborators, director/writer Michel Gondry and artist Pierre Bismuth (who both came up with the germ of the idea), one suspects that, most likely, Kaufman was simply relieved, appreciative, and anxious to get off the stage and step back into relative anonymity.

The film, directed by former musician/music video director Gondry (who will be discussed later in this book), is a hyper-realistic mélange of fantasy and science fiction, examining the achingly painful disintegration of a short but intense romantic relationship between two downwardly mobile New Yorkers, played by Jim Carrey (in what is undoubtedly his finest performance) and Kate Winslet, and the separate, wilful decisions made by both of them to literally erase the other one from the mind with a simple, cost-effective medical procedure. It is arguably Charlie Kaufman's crowning achievement so far as a screen-writer – certainly his most emotionally satisfying, nuanced work – and as close to perfection as any script can get.

He is our pre-eminent explorer of anxiety-laced inner space, a cross between Franz Kafka and Woody Allen, with a pinch of Larry David, a dollop or two of Philip K. Dick, and a huge slathering of Samuel Beckett sprinkled with Jorge Luis Borges to top it off. Kaufman is a post-modern, pathologically ambidextrous fantasist of the first order, a smiley-faced Bruno Schultz on acid. Quintessentially Jewish, American, and anarchic, he is provocatively, brutally honest about the fractured, painfully intransient search for meaning in a meaningless world. He is also just plain funny.

Although his medium is the motion picture screenplay, Kaufman's intricately structured narratives, explorations of fractured creative or cerebral protagonists manoeuvring through psychological morasses of self-hate while still desperately trying to connect with the people hovering around them, and his fearless ability to oscillate the tone of his scripts between meta-fictional fantasy, self-confessional kidney punches, outright funny punch lines and a plaintiveness that is completely touching without segueing into the maudlin for even a moment, are as complex and psychologically resonant as the best literary talents working today – as David L. Ulin, writer and book editor for the *Los Angeles Times*, pointed out in his excellent 2006 piece 'Why Charlie Kaufman is Us'.[5] Like many contemporary writers of the New Fantastic – people like Jonathan Lethem, Michael Chabon, Kelly Link, Jonathan Carroll, George Saunders, and Aimee Bender, among others – Kaufman navigates the subterranean psychological terrain within the fissures of our conscious reality with a dexterity that only a great storyteller can deliver. And also like the great storytellers of the weird and fantastic, Kaufman knows that the excursions into the surreal are only effective if as much imaginative fidelity is dedicated to realising the world of his characters – the ones slipping between the figurative cracks, or literally journeying through the head of John Malkovich for that matter – in concrete, resolutely naturalistic terms. It's got to be real… before it gets unreal.

For as long as the film medium has been around, screenwriter pure-bred kind, *not* director/writer combinations) have been batt out with directors and producers for artistic recognition. From the un- heralded silent film scenario writers to Anita Loos (the queen of silent film and early talkies sass and sophistication) to Ben Hecht (the first real superstar of Hollywood screenwriting), Nunnally Johnson, Preston Sturges, Dudley Nichols, Ring Lardner Jr, Dalton Trumbo, William Goldman, and Robert Towne, not to mention the flood of literary novelists and playwrights (Fitzgerald, Odets, Faulkner, Wodehouse, Parker) who have been attracted to Tinseltown ad nauseam because of the bountiful riches awaiting them – the Hollywood screenwriter has long (with rare exceptions) been the dog feeding on the foulest of scraps. And even when those scraps are good or at least nourishing, the fight for the last, bloody morsel is usually fraught with innumerable sacrifices regardless of the hefty paycheque at the bottom of the slop.

Charlie Kaufman is an exception – though as any working screenwriter, especially of the 'overnight sensation' variety, will inform you, the road to public recognition and artistic autonomy is a brutal one indeed. But the rise of Kaufman's star, and his rare, privileged position as the true *auteur* of his own films, is a feat which only a few screenwriters ever managed, and even then most of them – e.g. Preston Sturges – had to become directors as well to get it.

Notoriously shy and reluctant to speak about his private life – 'I don't like talking about myself,' he plainly stated in an interview for indieWIRE[6] – Kaufman was born in Long Island, New York, in 1958. In the *Salon* profile of the screenwriter, 'Being Charlie Kaufman',[7] Kaufman mentions that his hometown resembled the pre-fab designer suburb Levittown, a community that was intended as the archetypal neighbourhood of the future. But like David Lynch and the Coen Brothers before him, Kaufman was able to feel the strange currents flowing beneath the surface of all that suburban security and sanity.

The facts as we know them of his life are unremarkable. Relocating with his family to West Hartford, Connecticut, when he was a teenager, the young Kaufman attended William H. Hall High School to no great acclaim and graduated in 1976. As Enid (Thora Birch) from Terry Zwigoff's film *Ghost World* (2001) deadpans in response to a classmate's over-the-top exclamation, 'Yeah. We graduated high school. How... totally... amazing'. Following graduation, Kaufman moved to Boston, Massachusetts, and enrolled at Boston University for a short time before heading to New York City and attending NYU Film School. The young Kaufman always had a penchant for comedy (the Marx Brothers, the early Woody Allen, and Lenny Bruce), enjoyed the theatre, studied films, and read voraciously.

Nothing spectacular. Nothing out of the ordinary.

In contrast to what many of us probably assume about him, Kaufman's upbringing and artistic preoccupations seem to be no more outré or avant-garde than most late-American baby boomers inclined to the arts. But what *is* remarkable is how much the collective pop culture of post-WW II America – the films, the novels, the music, the comic books, the stand-up comedy routines – filtered down through his work, unlike many of his post-modern literary or cinematic contemporaries. Like the graceful, intelligent storyteller that Kaufman is, the residue of the culture around him, that permeated the very fabric of life in late twentieth-century America and that ebbed and flowed across the oceans, colouring the collective imaginations of anyone plugged into the pop-culture ether abroad, the influences are organic, hidden, embedded within the fabric of the story and the characters' lives. Kaufman's films are not movies about movies nor are they cultural regurgitations cynically spewing out the weird factor for the sake of being weird. Firmly grounded within character, story, and emotion, even when they are at their most fantastical, Kaufman's stories comprise the basic components of classic filmmaking despite their apparent lack of commercial viability. Surprisingly, though, his films routinely receive praise from both critics and audiences alike, dispelling increasingly antiquated attitudes about what mainstream audiences will or will not accept. As writer/director Quentin Tarantino proved in 1994 when his eccentric and gleefully profane second feature, the pseudo-indie *Pulp Fiction*, earned over $100,000,000 at the US box office and

garnered numerous prestigious awards including an Oscar for [
Original Screenplay, mainstream audiences *will* turn out for dark,
ficult, bizarre, or uncompromising films if they are grounded in classic
storytelling foundations.

After film school, Kaufman began to collaborate with a fellow classmate, Paul Proch (now a successful artist), on several projects, including numerous plays and screenplays that have, to this day, remained
far from the public eye. The two friends, though, eventually stumbled
upon some modest success when *National Lampoon* magazine agreed
to publish several of their faux 'Letters to the Editor' and other pieces
such as a Kurt Vonnegut parody, 'God Bless You, Mr Vonnegut'.[8]

In the late 1980s, Kaufman moved to Minneapolis, Minnesota, and
worked at the circulation desk of the *Star Tribune* newspaper where
he answered phone calls from irate subscribers who hadn't received
their morning issue. He also filled in at the Minneapolis Institute of
Arts while living in the city for the next four and a half years. During
this time, Kaufman and Proch managed to write a couple of on-spec
television scripts (which were never produced), most notably one for
the then-popular American sitcom, *Newhart*.

But Minneapolis was not going to be the place for the ambitious
Kaufman to break into Hollywood. In 1991, he drove out west to Los
Angeles – like countless others had done before him – attempting
to break into the industry. He landed an agent and eventually found
work writing for writer/actor Chris Elliot's short-lived television sitcom
Get a Life! (1991–92), which found the former writer for *Late Night
with David Letterman* as a 30-year-old paperboy living in his parents'
garage. The show lasted only two seasons. More jobs subsequently
came Kaufman's way and he ended up penning numerous episodes
for the short-lived television sketch comedy show *The Edge* (created
by David Mirkin, who had been an executive producer for *Newhart*, co-
creator of *Get a Life!* and would later work on *The Simpsons* for several years), which ran for two seasons (1993–94), and working on the
sitcoms *The Trouble with Larry* (1993) and *Ned and Stacy* (1996–97).
He also wrote for ex-*Saturday Night Live* comedian Dana Carvey's

absurdist sketch comedy show, *The Dana Carvey Show*, which aired on the ABC network in the spring of 1996 and featured future comedy stars Stephen Colbert and Steve Carrell in the cast.

For all intents and purposes, Charlie Kaufman was 'making it' in Hollywood. But despite the modest credits and success, he was not writing what truly mattered to him. That, of course, would be remedied when he ventured into the head of one of America's finest, most strangely seductive character actors, John Malkovich, exiting with one of the most peculiar and original screenplays to hit the screens in recent memory. An 'overnight sensation' was born.

After the critical and audience acclaim that followed *Being John Malkovich* (1999), Kaufman collaborated with directors Michel Gondry and Spike Jonze (again) on the films *Human Nature* (2001) and *Adaptation* (2002) respectively. He also wrote the screenplay *Confessions of a Dangerous Mind* (2003), based on the notorious (and highly improbable) autobiography of former television game show host and self-confessed CIA assassin Chuck Barris.

In 2003, in the wake of the success of *Adaptation*, rumours spread of Kaufman and Jonze re-teaming to work on an 'untitled horror project'.[9] Over the next few years, Kaufman would mention the untitled film during interviews, but nothing concerning the plot was known, other than that it was about the breakup of a relationship and that it would be 'scary' and 'creepy', though not disturbing in the traditional manner of horror films. The project eventually manifested into Kaufman's directorial debut *Synecdoche, New York* (2008), focusing on a middle-aged playwright named Caden, who suffers from a mysterious ailment and has plummeted into depression over his inability to create art with true meaning or insight. Desperately trying to keep his floundering marriage to a successful painter afloat while kindling a separate relationship with a young woman who works the theatre box office, Caden grows more neurotic and horrified at the thought of being washed up, undesirable, and ultimately alone. But when Caden begins a new play, an ambitious epic re-telling of his life in the moment – complete with a microcosmic rebuilding of the city of New

York as the setting of the 'play' – within the confines of an abandoned warehouse, his disintegrating personal life starts to become, if not completely clear to him, then perhaps a bit more meaningful, with the slight chance that he may discover a glimmer of truth before the onslaught of senility, madness, disease, and ultimately death snuffs him, and all of us, out.

The script (at least an early draft of it) is the boldest, riskiest, and most subtle exploration that Kaufman has yet undertaken, dealing with many of his favourite preoccupations – the war between body and mind, one's inability to see oneself clearly without a major personality cataclysm, and the need for creating art as a way for the protagonist to finally break through their own solipsism, a way for them to see through another's eyes, if only for a moment. Always an unpredictable writer, if Kaufman manages to translate a quarter of what is contained in the script to screen, it will be a major achievement. At 152 pages, it's an epic, surreal, depressing, and comedic chronicle of one man's personal apocalypse, one that approximates our own struggles within the mundane miraculous as well. Kaufman's themes of the value of art to the individual, the search for sexual and intellectual connection with another human being and our frequent unhappiness when and if we're lucky enough to get it, are also on fine display here. But there is also an added depth and emotional power to the script, a scope that seems to lift off directly from where he left off with *Eternal Sunshine of the Spotless Mind*. With its slipstream SF setting and incandescent through-the-looking-glass mix of James Joyce, Philip K. Dick, Terry Gilliam, Dennis Potter, and the very best of Fellini, *Synecdoche, New York* reads like Kaufman's masterwork, a tale about the 'human condition' in all its sadness, joy, humiliation, exuberance, defiance, and ultimate submission to the Great Equaliser awaiting us all.

Certainly a lot can change from words on the page to images flashed on a cinema screen. But that risk, that foolhardy need to test the waters swimming with sharks, is what makes Charlie Kaufman's talent even more impressive. Somehow, despite increasing success, awards, praise and acceptance from his peers, critics, and audiences alike, the worst creative sin of all – complacency – has not manifested in his work. His films are just as surprising, vibrant, and unpredictable now as when he first plunged us through Malkovich's inner being in 1999. Maybe even more so.

As of this writing, *Synecdoche, New York* has not been released or given a release date. Starring Philip Seymour Hoffman, Catherine Keener, Michelle Williams, Samantha Morton, Tom Noonan, and Jennifer Jason Leigh, the film will no doubt perplex, disturb, enchant and challenge filmgoers willing to work in tandem with a storyteller dedicated to delivering tales that refuse to talk down or insult our intelligence.

Embedded Within The Dream Factory: The (New) American New Wave

'There are no waves – new or old – there is only the ocean.'
– Claude Chabrol

The *nouvelle vague*, at least in those early films by Truffaut, Godard, Chabrol, Rohmer, and Rivette that flickered across the screens of the world, was primarily known for its technical and narrative experimentation, sophistication and playful rebelliousness. Those early cinematic provocations went on to influence countless other filmmakers and storytellers around the world, and for a moment young filmgoers felt as though cinema was speaking to them and their concerns. Filmmakers in Hollywood in the 1970s, influenced by their Gallic counterparts, attempted to infuse their own films with a similar attitude of experimentation and an agenda of stark realism and leftist politics in contrast to the conservative artistic status quo of the time. But the majority of these productions – however brilliant many of them were – failed to snap with the same laconic coolness that typified many of the early French films. The films of New Hollywood, though groundbreaking and influential in their own right, were far too cynical, downbeat, and caustic to make for an appropriate comparison to the *nouvelle vague*.

But eventually America would produce a group of filmmakers that exuded much of the same reckless artistry and many of the attributes that Truffaut and company initially championed. This new generation of mostly American filmmakers – Linklater, Anderson, Jonze, Coppola, Gondry (who is French, appropriately enough) – are not bound by any conscious aesthetic, philosophical, or political outlook, unlike the original *nouvelle vague* or even the Dogma 95 filmmakers were. There are, however, a number of unifying themes that have become apparent in their work since these American *enfants terribles* first arrived on the scene. Highly idiosyncratic yet intricately realised, accessible yet willing to overthrow the constraints of formal storytelling, surreal yet always grounded in human emotions, this new breed of American film captures the angst of its characters and the times in which we live, but with a wryness, imagination, earnestness, irony, and stylish wit that makes the slide into existential despair a little more amusing than it should be. By examining the pivotal films from the chief culprits in this undeclared war on reality, showing how this unique collective of creators infuse their modern fables with elements of fantasy, science fiction, and Surrealism, we can uncover a subtle, subversive element at work within the staid confines of the Hollywood dream factory.

Which is what a new wave is supposed to be, right? Subversive. Advanced. Brave and willing to tear down barriers, provoking us with ideas as much as with technique. A true progressive movement would never consciously mimic the stylistic advances made by earlier artists. It would never appropriate, embellish, slavishly imitate or mindlessly copy without forging its own aesthetic path. All of the filmmakers in this book *are* challenging the status quo, and most of them have done it while rooted within the Hollywood establishment or, at least, right outside its doors with an occasional inside job, like Linklater. None of them would ever be so cavalier as to say it's been easy. While the studios have been remarkably receptive to their idiosyncratic visions, there has also been plenty of trouble when some of these creators embark on pictures bloated with bigger budgets, egos, and risk – David O. Russell's *Three Kings* (1999), Wes Anderson's *The Life Aquatic with Steve Zissou* (2004), and Sofia Coppola's *Marie Antoinette* (2006) immediately come to mind.

This book is in no way intended as the last word on any of these filmmakers. It's merely an introduction, a doorway to further study, further inquiry into a significant band of outsiders who have managed to uphold their unique and peculiar cinematic visions in a factory town that seems content to interminably huff away on its own fumes. That is, until the next wave comes crashing down.

RICHARD LINKLATER

'As a filmmaker I trust that there is this core of people that I can communicate with. There's something inside people... If I'm honest with myself, there is a connection, people will respond to that. If you have to anticipate emotions, create them artificially, you're rudderless. Then you don't know, it's all hit and miss. "I *think* this will affect people emotionally," but if it doesn't affect *you* emotionally, you're dead.' – Richard Linklater[10]

Along with David O. Russell, director Richard Linklater is the conscience, the socially aware yet inwardly drawn soul of this loose collective of filmmakers. He is also America's finest, and least acknowledged, action-film director. The action may exist solely in the mind, but Linklater's consciousness-shifting drifters and vagabonds are always on the move telepathically, always searching for a new way to engage life below the radar and on their own terms. Whether Linklater is chronicling the not-so-passive, neo-bohemian slackers that populate Austin, Texas, burrowing deep within the troubled psyche of an undercover narcotics agent who is spying on himself, or going all family friendly with Jack Black being... well, Jack Black, Linklater is consistently examining the furrowed mindscape of contemporary American life in all its meandering stoner logic and increasingly worrying paranoia, suspicion, and apathy.

The Austin-based Linklater first arrived on the American independent film scene in 1991 with the release of *Slacker*, a deceptively wayward, low-budget art film that chronicled a day in the life of college town Austin and some of its roustabout, fringe-dwelling citizen-dreamers as they simultaneously fell away from yet aggressively engaged existence. The film was, along with Steven Soderbergh's *sex, lies, and videotape* (1989), a pivotal moment in the maturation of the so-called Sundance generation. If Linklater's film received far less critical praise (and awards) than Soderbergh's coolly-drawn suburban existential melodrama, time has been far kinder to Linklater's misfits than to Soderbergh's neurotics.

Linklater, who moved to Austin in the mid-1980s, had spent the early years of the Reagan decade somewhat attending an East Texas college, working as an offshore oil rigger, or doing what many aspiring filmmakers do before actually digging deep in the actual physical process of filmmaking – lazing about at his parents house and watching lots of films at the local cinema.[11] Eventually, though, the idea of making a low-budget film himself started to take hold while living in Austin. Like many a cinephile before (the *nouvelle vague* filmmakers and critics were integral members of film clubs while working for their respective film journals) and after him, Linklater co-founded his own film club in 1985. The Austin Film Society, a non-profit organisation dedicated to regional film, quality fringe cinema, and rarely seen classics, is still very much active today, listing Charles Burnett, Guillermo del Toro, Jonathan Demme, Mike Judge, Robert Rodriguez, Nancy Savoca, John Sayles, Steven Soderbergh, Paul Steckler, Quentin Tarantino, Elizabeth Avellan, and Kevin Smith among its board of advisers. And when not showcasing films, the AFS dedicates itself to overseeing the Austin Studios production facility, and supporting the work of regional directors, among other things.

Much like the DIY aesthetic of American hardcore punk bands such as Black Flag, The Dead Kennedys, Minor Threat, Husker Du, and countless others that roamed from college town to big city back to college town in rundown vans just to play their music with little or no regard for commercial viability, Linklater gambled everything on realising his first foray into feature filmmaking, *Slacker*. The ultra-low-budget film, after weathering plenty of shrugs and confusion from festival programmers and critics alike, would eventually earn over $1,000,000 from an estimated cost of $23,000. Not too bad for a film where supposedly nothing happens.

With the success of *Slacker*, Linklater went on to make the underrated *Dazed and Confused* (1993), a thoughtful, funny, teenage reminiscence set on the last day of school circa 1976 that eschewed many of the typical clichés found in the American high school subgenre and took a laid-back free ride to a past that has been horrifyingly misremembered and cloyingly sentimentalised by films and television shows alike. The film, distributed by Gramercy Pictures (a subsidiary of Universal Pictures), was dumped into the box-office trough and, unsurprisingly, did not perform well. But over the years the film, which launched a number of future stars or screen favourites such as Ben Affleck, Matthew McConaughey, Milla Jovovich, Joey Lauren Adams, Parker Posey, and Adam Goldberg to name just a few, has entered the cult zone and is arguably a bona fide stoner classic that has plenty of depth swirling through its green haze.

Next came the intimate two-character romance, *Before Sunrise* (1995), starring Ethan Hawke and Julie Delpy, detailed in depth later in this book. A year on Linklater returned to an ensemble cast when he collaborated with New York City-based actor/playwright Eric Bogosian for the 1997 film *subUrbia*, which centred on a group of wayward 20-somethings who become even more emotionally dissolute when a former comrade (now a rock star) from their group returns to the teenage wasteland of deserted parking lots, convenience stores, and fastfood joints, further turning a boring night into an irretrievably bad one. Starring Giovanni Ribisi, Nicky Katt, Steve Zahn, and Parker Posey, the film is a far more cynical and darker view of the lost years of youth than Linklater's earlier films (no doubt because the script was written by Bogosian based on his play, though Linklater *did* work closely with him on the adaptation) and reviews were generally kind. Janet Maslin of the *New York Times* found the film 'toxically satirical'[12] and felt that 'its murderous mix of junk food, wasted time, petty envy and gallows humor... [created]... a truly ghostly view...'[13] of its desolate locale.

The *Los Angeles Times* critic Jack Mathews, on the other hand, felt that Linklater was treading old ground in his fourth film and that it was 'darker and nastier'[14] than the material we had become accustomed to from the cautiously optimistic Truffaut from Austin.

One doesn't usually think of historical films when Linklater's name comes up, but the director had long harboured a desire to make a film about the infamous though genial Newton Boys, who robbed banks and trains through North America in the early part of the twentieth century and never once fired a shot. Starring Matthew McConaughey, Skeet Ulrich, Ethan Hawke, and Vincent D'Onofrio, the film was Linklater's first substantially budgeted film ($27,000,000) and an opportunity for him to branch out further and show that he wasn't just the guy who made films about college-age slackers. Audiences, unfortunately, stayed away. But some astute critics, namely Jonathan Rosenbaum from the *Chicago Reader*, proclaimed that the film might be Linklater's *Jules et Jim* and praised the film's 'astonishing handling of period detail and its gentleness of spirit'.[15] Almost ten years on, the film seems ripe for reappraisal.

Linklater's experimental animated film *Waking Life* (detailed later) arrived three years later. The digitally shot, three-character drama *Tape* was also released in 2001 (just a few weeks after *Waking Life*), based on the seedy play by Steven Belber, starring Ethan Hawke, Uma Thurman, and Robert Sean Leonard.

In 2003, Linklater would direct his friend Timothy 'Speed' Levitch, who was the subject of the 1998 documentary *The Cruise* directed by Bennett Miller (*Capote*) and would have an equally memorable, though shorter, role in *Waking Life*, in the short film *Live from Shiva's Dance Floor*. Linklater would also surprise many by doing the impossible. Not because he didn't have the talent, of course, but because very few would have dared to believe that his next film, *School of Rock* (2003), would become a major hit. Not a blockbuster perhaps, but impressive enough that the film's success would serve him well with many in Hollywood for years to come. Written by Mike White – who penned and starred in the indie-favourite *Chuck & Buck* (2000) – and starring

Jack Black, the family-friendly comedy extolling the virtues of rock in all its blistering aural confections is far from the 'sell-out' many feared and a perfect showcase for a comedic actor who had rarely been better in feature films. There's a genuine sense of rowdy esprit to it. It's also a film well aware of the 'cute kid' nausea threshold, managing to thankfully pull back from any embarrassments. A strange yet welcome diversion for the filmmaker.

Linklater, Hawke, and Delpy returned to the characters from *Before Sunrise* with a sequel set some ten years on. The film, *Before Sunset* (2004), is equally rewarding – maybe even more so. Another family-friendly film followed in 2005, this time a remake of Michael Richie's *Bad News Bears*, starring Billy Bob Thornton in the role of Buttermaker, the alcoholic and cigar-chomping Little League Baseball manager originally made famous by Walter Matthau. Unlike the successful *School of Rock*, the film barely broke even. Following this in 2006, Linklater made two of his most interesting and timely films, *A Scanner Darkly* and *Fast Food Nation*.

Currently, the filmmaker is undertaking his most ambitious project – *Boyhood*. Though he started filming in 2001, the film will not be finished or seen until 2013 as it chronicles the raising of a child from the age of six to eighteen years of age. Linklater and his principal actors – Patricia Arquette and Ethan Hawke as the parents, Ellar Salmon as their son – meet once a year to film their 'story', blurring the lines between reality and fiction in the hope of capturing that elusive 'holy moment', a term used by Linklater in *Waking Life* to describe André Bazin's theory concerning the possibility that film could be a spiritually transformative experience and that the camera is sometimes able to seize on a beautiful flash of truth within the illusion.

Slacker (1991) & Waking Life (2001)

Directed by: Richard Linklater
Written by: Richard Linklater
Produced by: Richard Linklater (Slacker); Tommy Pallota, Jonah Smith,

Anne Walker-McBay, Palmer West (Waking Life)
Edited by: Scott Rhodes (Slacker); Sandra Adair (Waking Life)
Cinematography by: Lee Daniels (Slacker); Richard Linklater, Tommy Pallota (Waking Life)
Cast: a whole slew of slackers, dreamers, and mostly non-actors

'Uh, I don't do much really, I just read, and work here, and, uh, sleep and eat, and, uh, watch movies.' – The Anti-Artist states his role in the grand mystery of it all in *Slacker*.

'Resistance is not futile, we're gonna win this thing, humankind is too good, we're not a bunch of under-achievers! We're gonna stand up, and we're gonna be human beings. We're going to get fired up about the real things, the things that matter! Creativity and the dynamic human spirit that refuses to submit.' – Firebrand Alex Jones likewise states his case in *Waking Life*.

Slacker is a film that frustrates, mystifies, and bores as many people as it charms others, who find within its absurdist, meandering soul a cinematic reflection of their own under-the-radar college years, or who can relate in some way to the film's ensemble of open books, so to speak, who are tripping, bickering, loafing, but, more importantly, philosophising their way through life. The camera floats around these self-styled Oblomovs, these conjurors of reality, as they impress their uncensored worldviews upon anyone who brushes into their solipsist fantasies, and Linklater – in a hallmark of most of his films – never passes judgement. Not that any of these characters, relegated to purgatory within the margins of anyone else's script, could care less what anyone thought about them.

From the first character that we see – the guy on the bus, played by Linklater, who jumps in a cab and begins inundating the driver with talk of a strange dream he just had about the possibility of a single thought sparking an alternate reality right around the corner – to the final joyous moments when one of a group of youths, equipped with the necessary equipment for documenting life in the moment (Super 8 cameras), gleefully hurls his machine over the cliff, thereby reminding us that life does indeed exist beyond the frame, *Slacker* is a showcase of people seeking to infuse their lives with meaning. You may not always agree or even like many of the wildly disparate flock of over-and-under-achieving ne'er-do-wells that crowd this 100-minute film, but you have to respect them as they maintain mental sobriety beyond the fringe. As one character, the slightly menacing hitchhiker (Charles Gunning), boasts to a small film crew about his seemingly wayward existence, 'Look at me. I'm making it. I may live badly, but at least I don't have to work to do it'. Not surprisingly, many of the film's most vehement detractors would claim otherwise.

Linklater's *La Ronde*-styled (sans interlocutor) carousel of wanderers, missing persons, JFK conspiracy theoreticians, aging anarchists, jaded lovers, matricide-minded, beetle-eyed Boy Scouts, shut ins, and other assorted 'everyday people' was first hatched in the mid-1980s, after he had moved to Austin and began doing what any young aspiring filmmaker does if he or she wants to 'break into' the film industry – make films. And Linklater made plenty of them. Mostly they were experimental short film endeavours that were meant to teach him technique and sharpen what directorial skills he had picked up from a steady diet of watching and dissecting films (classic European art house, experimental, and a heavy slab of good ol' prime American cinema), and from reading books on film theory and directors. He was consumed by film, and as Linklater stated in the commentary for his first feature, the Super 8-lensed *It's Impossible to Learn to Plow by Reading Books*, his life outside of film was a 'void'.[16]

Plow was completed in 1988 and cost around $3,000. It is a curious and confused amalgam of low-rent American existentialism by way of avant-garde filmmakers such as James Benning and the New German Cinema from the 1970s, especially Wim Wenders' adaptation of Peter Handke's novel *Die Angst des Tormanns beim Elfmete/ The Goalkeeper's Fear of the Penalty* (1972), documentary, and experimental underground cinema. The meandering narrative focuses on an unnamed protagonist, played by Linklater, who wanders around his hometown, hops a train and rides up to Montana to stay with a friend, hangs out, and eventually wanders back home where it can be realistically argued that either he or his more verbal doppelganger eventually trips out of the frame of his own story and into the cosmic celluloid mélange of Linklater's breakthrough film. It is in fact possible that the philosophising traveller at the beginning of *Slacker* is indeed the same character. Linklater would again make an appearance in a similar role at the beginning of *Waking Life*.

Plow definitely has some tantalising moments – Linklater's character leaving a note for a sleeping young woman he had spent some time with at the train station – and a strange moment when the shirtless unnamed man fires a rifle out of the top storey of his house before embarking on his trip, a significant narrative jolt to say the least. But Linklater refuses to wander down the narrative path of turning our protagonist into some deadpan spree killer, a low-rent Charles Whitman. A narrative like that was not of interest to the then-emerging filmmaker, and though subsequent films would adhere more closely to traditional dramatic structure, Linklater has always been an affable anti-structuralist (not in a strict academic sense) and has always favoured the capricious verbal sauntering that flows from dialogue and character over plot contrivances.

But despite *Plow*'s flaws, it was a significant marker in the cinematic evolution of Linklater, and would serve him well when he burrowed deeper into the more ambitious *Slacker*. The latter's loose structure and fondness for camera takes that never centre on one character for too long built upon the lessons learned from the earlier film and expanded *Plow*'s vague ideas about isolation and alienation. Unlike the nameless drifter in *Plow*, who really is empty inside and does not feel any real urgency *to* connect with anyone outside of his own head, the characters in *Slacker* cannot stop attempting to connect, much to the dismay of the person being assaulted by whatever emerging reality is crashing down upon them.

Slacker was not an immediate success on the independent film circuit. The Sundance Film Festival initially rejected the film when it was still a work-in-progress (although the film was shown there once it was completed in 1991 and nominated for the Grand Jury Prize), and other festivals such as the Toronto Film Festival were also dismissive. Eventually, though, it did find an appreciative audience via an exuberant reception at the Seattle Film Festival and subsequently an article in *Film Comment*,[17] which found its way to the influential indie-film representative, John Pierson. Pierson, a legendary figure on the independent film scene of the late 1980s and early 1990s, and the author of the book *Spike, Mike, Slackers & Dykes*, chronicling his decade in the trenches of the then-creative and financially blossoming independent scene, got word about Linklater's film, scooped it up, and eventually sold it to Orion Classics. Pretty soon, Linklater's cinematic love letter to the losers, freaks, and under-achieving misfits of the world would, for a brief moment, spiral its way into the public consciousness, reintroduce a word into the mass lexicon, and represent a joyously crazy voice from the maladjusted underground. The pop culture party above ground was about to be crashed.

In 2001, Richard Linklater returned to the dreamers of Austin – though the film, much like Linklater's slipstream narrative, stretches farther than any geographical limitations – utilising a vibrantly expressive 'interpolating rotoscope' technique similar to what Disney captured in *Snow White and the Seven Dwarves* (1933) and animation director Ralph Bakshi used in his relatively family friendly (this was, after all, the director of the notorious adult cartoons *Fritz the Cat* and *Coonskin*) counter-culture fantasy epic *Wizards* (1977), and his 1978 version of *The Lord of the Rings*. But unlike Bakshi's use of the rotoscoping technique, wherein an artist traces over an already filmed moving object – in the case of *Wizards*, sequences lifted from Sergei Eisenstein's historical epic *Alexander Nevsky* (1938) and Anthony Mann's *El Cid* (1961), among others – *Waking Life*'s approach to the technique was meant to be more fluid and expressive visually than anything ever attempted before.

Art director and MIT grad Bob Sabiston, creator of the Rotoshop software and head of the animation production company Flat Back

Films, and his crew of 30 graphic artists were determined to elevate *Waking Life* a touch or two off the ground, much as Wiley Wiggins' dream adventurer lifts off his bed and through the roof of his bedroom in the film. Once Linklater had filmed the entire script on digital video, the animators then traced the actors with light pens and processed the scenes using the Rotoshop software. Scenes were then manipulated, layered, and enhanced to give shots a sort of floating, shifting, impressionistic 3-D effect. The technique would be even more advanced in Linklater's later film *A Scanner Darkly*, casting an even more hyperrealistic – and decidedly darker – dream world of America.

Like *Slacker*, the plot is simple and threadbare, but the excursion through it is dynamic and exhilarating at times. Basically a journey through a myriad of 'past and current trends in philosophy'[18] as encountered by a nameless young man played by Wiley Wiggins, of *Dazed and Confused* fame, the film uses animation as a means to lull the viewer into a state of lucid participatory viewing, sometimes literally visualising abstract, difficult concepts in a playful, humourous, and seemingly improvisatory manner. This is film as jazz: wild, communicative, conceptual, and joyful. But unlike the free-form Sub-Genius[19] slackers in the earlier film, the raconteurs here are more so than not attempting to elucidate on real philosophical theories, though the homespun webs of basement theorising are ever-present as well. Buddhism, Taoism, Existentialism, Situationism, Semiotics, André Bazin's theory of film as 'holy moment' as conveyed by indie filmmaker Caveh Zahedi – one of the film's stand-out moments – and New Evolution/AI concepts are all transmuted into visual action.[20]

But for all of the film's whimsical, cerebral tango sessions, the stain of human suffering, confusion, and mental enslavement is never far off. One of the film's most startling and memorable moments comes in the form of an incarcerated, demonically enraged Charles Gunning (is this perhaps a parallel version of his black-clad drifter from *Slacker*?) spewing forth his sadistic ideas of revenge of 'living Hell' upon the judge, the psychiatrist, and everyone else who put him behind bars. His energy is poisonous and horrifying to contemplate, but there is a strange Blakean logic to it (he is after all only following his true nature) as he prowls up and down within his personal Seventh Circle of Hell.

It's not every day that a major Hollywood studio – Twentieth Century Fox in this case – finances a treatise on free will, conspiracy theories, resistance against corporate slavery, 'liminal frontier moments', and the need for people to wake up and ask themselves a simple but confounding question: What will you do with your life in the moment? Whether the film focuses on 'real human moments', as one character late in the film plaintively yearns for and requests from our nameless main character, or complex theories espoused by philosophy professors wryly asking us – the viewers – to examine whether or not humans are indeed actually unique or simply a form of 'super ape', Linklater offers to us something that has become increasingly rare in modern American commercial filmmaking: an intellectual engagement with the filmmaker and with his characters; a resistance to the norm and an exit from passive viewership. His characters embrace real action, respond to new ideas, differing opinions and display a willingness to be open to possibilities beyond their awareness.

Linklater, for all his contemplative coffee-house demeanour, is an action filmmaker in the truest sense because he dares us to walk away from two hours of seeming passivity and engage life on new terms. *Waking Life*, more than any of his films up to this point, allows us to reclaim curiosity within the wellspring of ideas and with cinema itself. Like a shape-shifting Coltrane solo, *Waking Life* flows toward currents of meaning upon a love supreme of images, ideas, and a symmetry of emotion. It is a fluid manifesto of wakefulness, a dream within a dream, intricately sublime as much as it is ridiculous, tedious, and overwhelming. But within its magic frames a squiggly revolution of sorts awaits, a plea for viewers to remain open to the idea that reality is not as defined, not as rigid as we sometimes believe. In an age when the sad, mechanised and incurious Hollywood studio system seems ever more content to simply recycle, reconstitute and regurgitate what has come before, a film like *Waking Life* is something worth celebrating, even when it risks coming off as ridiculous or painfully earnest.

Before Sunrise (1995) & Before Sunset (2004)

Directed by: Richard Linklater
Written by: Richard Linklater, Kim Krizan (Before Sunrise); Richard Linklater, Kim Krizan, Julie Delpy, Ethan Hawke (Before Sunset)
Produced by: Anne Walker-McBay
Edited by: Sandra Adair
Cinematography by: Lee Daniel
Cast: Ethan Hawke, Julie Delpy, Dominic Castell

'I know happy couples… but I think they lie to each other.'
– Jesse (Ethan Hawke) in *Before Sunrise*

'The concept is absurd. The idea that we can only be complete with another person is evil. Right?' – Céline (Julie Delpy) in *Before Sunset*

It begins in motion, like many of Linklater's films, this time on a train somewhere in old Europa bound for Paris. A young woman, Céline (Julie Delpy), has been visiting her grandmother in Budapest and is returning to Paris where she studies at the Sorbonne. A young American man, named Jesse (Ethan Hawke), is journeying to Vienna where he intends to reluctantly jet back the next day to his home in the United States of Amnesia. The young couple, who are seated on either side of the aisle from one another, are both lost in their solitary worlds reading; Jesse is plowing through Klaus Kinski's insidiously readable autobiography, *Kinski: All I Need is Love* (aka *Kinski Uncut*), and Céline is reading an anthology by the equally notorious cultural destabiliser, Georges Bataille. Jesse and Céline are strangers to one another. But soon, due to a loud, bickering, middle-aged German couple seated near them – who eventually storm out of the car acting out a scene that has probably become a depressing clockwork ritual for them, much to the baffled, slightly contemptuous amusement of the two 20-somethings – Jesse introduces himself to the girl and, before you can say love at first sight, their real journey begins.

But the story does not *really* begin like that. At least, not with the 'love at first sight' bit. There is an attraction, to be sure, though nothing more dramatic than any other moment of their lives up to that point. There are no saccharine strings cascading on the soundtrack, determined to slosh the viewer in a head-freeze of schmaltz, no disharmonious attempts at forced witticism or charred, cynical charm passing as seductive intelligence. There is simply a glance, a mundane recognition and a discreet smile that for Jesse, who seems a bit distracted by the Germans' tumult, means an opportunity for talk.

The natural awkward rhythms of speech between these two people, who just seconds before were complete strangers, is captured with all of the relaxed insight and intelligence that has made Linklater's work so unique in American film. The camera, courtesy of the director's longtime cinematographer (and former roommate) Lee Daniel, unobtrusively observes the two as they work through the awkwardness of first meeting, then as they wander the streets of Vienna after Jesse convinces Céline that he isn't a 'psycho', but more significantly when he plays out for her a possible future scenario of discontented married life, as she wonders all the while whether she made the right decision getting off the train.

Thankfully, for anyone who loves intelligent dialogue and actors who are given the freedom to breathe, to ferret out the nuances of their characters' physicality, *Before Sunrise* is a balm of modest wisdom, as is its companion piece made nine years later, *Before Sunset*. The script, written by Linklater and Kim Krizan, and the interplay between the actors, allows the rhythms of the dialogue to flow regardless of the content, which ranges from the superficial to the existential, sometimes within the same scene, much like it does in 'real life'. This approximation of real speech, for which Linklater has consistently strived throughout his career, has never been more succinct or entrancing as in these two films. Both characters frequently contradict themselves, are disingenuous and often guarded about giving away too much.

Although lacking a conscious literary influence, both films are in love with language, trusting in the ability of words to truly convey the complexity of the inner self. Jesse and Céline likewise have faith in the power of language and aren't afraid to wield their vocabularies as enticement or shield. They're unafraid also to verbalise innumerable questions at one another, to risk being laughed at or ridiculed, because as Céline says at one point, 'the answer must be in the attempt'.

Sometimes, though, the silence between the two says much more, as the scene in the record-store listening booth sublimely conveys or at the end of the film when we see a series of quick shots showing us the empty places – an alleyway, a closed café, a solitary street, a quiet amusement park, the riverbank, the park where they made love – that Jesse and Céline inhabited hours before, a scene that delicately evokes a similar moment in Demy's *Les Parapluies de Cherbourg* before that film's lovers were divided by war and time. It's a haunting, lyrical moment, one that perfectly captures Jesse and Céline's heartbreak as well as their joy at having moved through these places together.

Before Sunset is equally entrancing. In the first film, our two companions were more or less beginning their adult lives, both still attending universities. Jesse, the more romantic, and, for all his projected cynicism, the softer one, still had the belief that his carefree (American) attitude would protect him through his middle-age; well-educated Céline, opinionated and more pragmatic, already seemed more worldly and slightly more impatient for her adulthood to begin, as if it would temper her more strident and neurotic characteristics. But nine years on, despite the obvious and inevitable changes of life in their 30s, Jesse and Céline immediately pick up where they left off.

Unlike the poignant final images of the first film, Linklater begins *Before Sunset* with a series of places that our two reunited lovers haven't yet engaged with, though they are far from being empty. Life and movement – people – fill the streets, sidewalks, parks and cafés that will eventually become the setting for the film. The melancholic tone that infused the end of *Before Sunrise* has vanished. Here, we have springtime in Paris, a perfect symbolic opportunity for a friendship to bloom in an entirely different manner than our two lovers had no doubt intended.

Jesse, now a novelist, married, and a father, is in Paris on the last day of his European book tour. His book, a *roman à clef* about their brief encounter, is a minor success. Céline works as an environmental activist and is in a 'good' long-term relationship with a photojournalist. Although Jesse only has 80 minutes before he has to arrive at the airport to catch a plane back to the States, they agree to spend the rest of the afternoon together, walking, and, of course, talking.

After some initial awkwardness (Jesse still seems intimidated by Céline's intelligence; she still seems confused by his naïveté), the two slip back into their communicative habits. Jesse isn't as youthfully romantic as he once was, but his optimism is still more or less intact. Céline is more pessimistic, angrier though still impassioned enough to try and do something about it. Life in all its complexity has blemished their idealism, but in essence they are still very much the same people they were nine years ago, though a little wiser, a little more battle hardened.

But the question in everyone's mind is: did they meet again in Vienna six months later, as they'd agreed to do on the train platform? Céline admits that she couldn't due to her grandmother's funeral. Jesse initially says that he couldn't make it either, but the pain and disappointment eventually breaks through the tension and he sheepishly admits that he did fly back to Vienna to rekindle their one night together.

If there was any trepidation that a 'sequel' to the first film was a bad idea, such fears are doused early on. It's impossible to say whether *Before Sunset* is a better film than its predecessor. But, together, the two films chart a unique and thoroughly rich portrait of friendship and love intertwined with the messiness of memories, regret, missed opportunities and the acceptance that life does not always end up the way you thought it would. And plenty *has* changed, though their core selves and attraction to one another haven't.

The film transposes events from the earlier film, showing how even the most minute gesture or initially insignificant comment can creep back via the unconscious as one's own. In the first film, Jesse mocked Céline's interest in New Age explanations such as reincarnation. Now he's obsessed with such ideas, unlike her. Céline, who was obviously pained and confused by having to leave Jesse on the train platform, simultaneously seemed – at least on an unconscious level – to be preparing herself to forget him, to file him away within her memory. Now she's haunted by her memories, perhaps because she hasn't yet dealt with them, unlike Jesse, who wrote a book about his heartbreak and in effect purged his disappointment over the matter, or at least eased the pain a little. Céline even admits that she's bothered by what Jesse wrote in the book and that she doesn't even remember them having sex in the park, though later on she talks about never forgetting the men she's been involved with... and later, that of course she remembered. It's too painful not to. And in direct relation to a seemingly fleeting moment from the first film – a scene in which Jesse attempts to tenderly touch Céline's hair, unbeknownst to her – Céline reaches out to touch Jesse in the same manner while he's not looking. The emotional undercurrents run deep, and with deeper longing for what could've been, regret being the great undercurrent of the film.

In lesser hands, both films would have been unwatchable. Unable to deal with the sometimes emotional irresolution of their dilemma, one can easily imagine how the film could have detoured in so many unsatisfactory ways. But Linklater and his two collaborators, Delpy and Hawke (all three were nominated for an Oscar for Adapted Screenplay), stay true to their characters and their frustrations – for they are miserable. Not just without each other, but because they realise only too well that life has a tendency to beat the hell out of you.

By the end, though, with Céline dancing unselfconsciously to Nina Simone in her kitchen while Jesse, seated on the couch, looks on, there is no mistaking that they are about to make up for those long nine years. It's a beautifully satisfying ending, perhaps the finest moment in any Linklater film. And a scene of such perfection that it almost scours from the memory the years of abuse Hollywood has inflicted upon the world with untruths in regard to romance. Before Sunset, as with Lost in Translation, Eternal Sunshine of the Spotless Mind and to a lesser extent Punch-Drunk Love – all released within a year or so of one another – is a clear example of how not every modern Hollywood film with an inclination toward affairs of the heart need be deceitful, sentimental or lacking in courage.

A Scanner Darkly (2006)

Directed by: Richard Linklater
Written by: Richard Linklater
Produced by: Tommy Pallotta, Jonah Smith, Erwin Stoff, Anne Walker-McBay, Palmer West
Edited by: Sandra Adair
Cinematography by: Shane F. Kelly
Cast: Keanu Reeves, Robert Downey, Jr., Woody Harrelson, Winona Ryder, Rory Cochrane

'It was fun to be in the realm of science fiction, but my jumping-off point was more *Alphaville* than anything else.' – Richard Linklater[21]

One would not immediately think of Richard Linklater to helm a science fiction film – unless, of course, it happened to be a science fiction film based on a novel by the late Philip K. Dick. The California-based writer, who died in 1982 just a few months before the release of Ridley Scott's film *Blade Runner* (adapted from Dick's 1966 novel *Do Androids Dream of Electric Sheep?*), was known for his prolific output and for his sardonic wit, corrosive satire, paranoia, narratives exploring the fragility of one's faith in the solidity of reality, and great empathy for the world's downtrodden misfits, drug addicts, or for anyone simply trying to get out of this beautifully troubled and perplexing reality without making too many ripples. Although plenty of Dick's novels and stories have reached the screen over the decades – from the futuristic noir of Scott's film to French director Jerome (*Baxter*) Boivin's *Confessions d'un Barjo* (1992) to Steven Spielberg's *Minority Report* (2002) – the less said about the majority of them the better. Most of the adaptations, *Barjo* excluded (the film is based on one of Dick's mainstream first novels, *Confessions of a Crap Artist*), routinely discard the author's psychological and metaphysical insights and instead bombard the viewer with an endless succession of thrilling chases, larger-than-life violent set pieces and simplistic, illogical narrative trickery that is supposed to replace the nuanced, absurd, terrifying, and sometimes very funny metaphysical shenanigans that plague Dick's main characters.

Linklater's film is by far the most faithful Dick adaptation yet attempted – the first to really capture the druggy mirth and misrule of the damaged souls Dick perpetually wrote about – and the most attuned to the sadness, paranoia, and absurdity contained in many of the books. Unsurprisingly, the film was authorised by the Philip K. Dick Trust. And by using a similar though more sophisticated version of the interpolated rotoscoping technique utilised in *Waking Life*, the film is a rarity among contemporary American animated films – an animated film for adults. No wisecracking animals, no sassy, acerbic, anthropomorphic dancin' critters need apply. This is animation that recalls the surreal, naturalistic yet imaginative works of Japanese animators such as Isao Takahata (*Grave of the Fireflies*) and Satoshi Kon (*Perfect Blue, Three Godfathers, Paprika*) more than it does the wildly fantastical, science fiction grit and gleam of, say, *Akira* or the films of the great Hayao Miyazaki.

Set 'seven years from now', the film has smartly updated the novel's Orange County, California setting circa 1994 – a post-1960s suburban wasteland of friendly fascism and mundane police-state tyranny wherein the shadow of President Richard Nixon still beams down with an insidious power – to the equally dystopian Bush-era civil liberties stampede which has run riot during his reign. This is the post-9/11 America of private security forces, private prisons, CCTV surveillance, the War on Drugs, legal pharmaceutical addiction, servitude to corporations, and, most disturbingly, compliance with the unwritten code of snitch culture and the willingness to put thy neighbour behind bars, if need be, for the good of the State Bureaucracy… and your neighbour. It is also the era of Substance D, aka Slow Death, a highly addictive hallucinogen/stimulant that also unleashes crippling paranoia and psychosis.

Within this sunshine-baked wonderland of law and order, undercover narcotics agent Bob Arctor (Keanu Reeves) has been assigned to embed himself within a household of Substance D users, played by

Robert Downey Jr. and Woody Harrelson, and eventually root out their main supplier. But to fit in convincingly with the group, Arctor must also become a user of Substance D, which ultimately serves as his physical, spiritual, and psychological downfall. He grows close to his friends and also gets involved with a woman named Donna (Winona Ryder), who is a cocaine addict and Arctor's supplier of Substance D. Eventually, the drug warps and destroys Arctor's ability to perceive a sole 'objective reality' (a common thread through all of Dick's work) and he quickly, painfully, succumbs to the drug's tyranny as well as becoming a pawn of the authoritarian police force he serves.

Neither the novel nor the film's strength lies with the plot. It is a framework that has been utilised in countless crime films or television shows. But here, the unsettling twist comes in the guise of a true existential paradox – what happens when the investigator has to investigate himself? Routinely called into the office to brief his superiors, Arctor (who is known as Officer Fred to his colleagues) masks his physical identity by wearing something called a scramble suit, a sort of hyper-kinetic electronic cloaking device that continuously flashes and morphs a multitude of visages upon the outer layer of the suit, effectively keeping the wearer's real face and voice a secret to the outside world. Predictably, Arctor's earnest yet quixotic attempt to investigate himself is marked by trouble, pain, and ultimately tragedy.

His brain fried, Arctor winds up at one of the many New Path rehabilitation centres that will help him lose his addiction to Substance D, seemingly dead to the world. But the film does offer us a cautious glimmer of hope in its final images, when the scoured husk of Arctor mindlessly works in the fields at one of New Path's many farms and slowly realises that the company has been a front for the harvesting and distribution of the very drug it supposedly combats. The zombiefied Arctor pockets one of the blue flowers that are the origin of Substance D, giving us at least a glimmer of hope that he will eventually deliver the evidence to the police.

Linklater's erudite, wonky, benevolent slackers are now burn-outs, willing victims of their own addiction, their own consumption and their own apathy. Arctor and his druggie compatriots have intentionally cho-sen to exist on the touchlines, dealing drugs (at least in Donna's case) because it's better than working some low-paying clerical job or, God forbid, a fast food joint (see next section). Besides, not having to work a dead-end job gives the bunch more time to hang out, discuss the problems of the world and ultimately ignore them.

Many of Dick's novels dealt with and/or attempted to transpose the effects of hallucinogens or other psychoactive drugs upon the mental states, though *A Scanner Darkly* was the first novel he wrote clean of drugs – his drug of choice for many years was doctor-prescribed methamphetamines. Nevertheless, *A Scanner Darkly* was Dick's most brutal and negative depiction of the destruction wrought by hard drugs upon the user, how they peel away at one's psyche until only the raw, frayed nerves are exposed. And while Linklater offers up a balanced view of drug use – from the seduction and tricksterish frivolity of life under the influence to the inevitable downward slide into cognitive dis-sociation, paranoia and death – the film never feels like a reckless ode to drug use or a reactionary attack. The wreckage of so many simply needs no embellishment.

Like the novel, the film ends with a tender postscript dedicated to the 'comrades' that '…wanted to keep on having a good time for-ever, and were punished for that'. And as the book was a product of its time, so is Linklater's film. Sinister, paranoiac undercurrents flow through the film, sometimes emanating from the characters' own psy-chosis – especially in the case of Freck, played by Rory Cochrane, who was equally memorable in Linklater's *Dazed and Confused* – while it could be said that the reason so many people are crawling into the darkness of their addictions is because it seems like the only sane response to a society in decline.

Fast Food Nation (2006)

Directed by: Richard Linklater
Written by: Eric Schlosser, Richard Linklater

Produced by: Malcolm McLaren, Jeremy Thomas
Edited by: Sandra Adair
Cinematography by: Lee Daniel
Cast: Patricia Arquette, Paul Dano, Mitch Baker, Luis Guzmán, Ethan Hawke, Ashley Johnson, Greg Kinnear, Kris Kristofferson, Avril Lavigne, Catalina Sandino Moreno, Lou Taylor Pucci, Ana Claudia Talancón, Wilmer Valderrama, Bruce Willis

'There's shit in the meat.' – Mickey's President Jack Deavers (Frank Ertl) stating the facts

As with the best crime films, which is essentially what Richard Linklater's film is, there are no easy roads to the truth and no convenient exit strategies once we get there. Released only a few months after *A Scanner Darkly*, Linklater's follow-up is equally complex, politicised and vital in its examination of a culture on the verge of eating itself to death. Using Eric Schlosser's bestselling exposé of the American fast food industry as a jumping-off point, the film adaptation develops and personalises the ideas explored in Schlosser's book by giving us several characters – from across the economic, gender and age spectrum – connected through their relationship to the fictional fast food chain, Mickey's.

In 2004, Linklater had written and directed an HBO prospective pilot entitled *$5.15/Hr*, starring William Lee Scott and then-unknown America Ferrera. Focusing on a group of mostly young people working the late shift at a family-style restaurant called Grammaw's Kitchen, the show would have chronicled the ups and downs of these individuals, ranging from the arrogant ladies' man played by Scott to the cringe-inducing eagerness of the Ferrera character, as they try to pay bills, raise children and stay a few inches above the troubled waters of debt, disillusionment and despair. The pilot, which was an honest and sometimes humorous attempt to show how some members of the true working class do live and work in the US, was not picked up by the cable network due to its 'depressing' tone. Although it would have been interesting to see what Linklater would have done with the material over the course of several episodes, no doubt much of the material trickled down to *Fast Food Nation*, which shares a similar though far more developed focus and tone.

Whether focusing on the Hispanic workers who are smuggled across the southern border into the US by human traffickers known as coyotes and who will eventually find work at a cattle-slaughtering processing plant, the teenagers who work at the fast food restaurant that ultimately serves up the food, or the behind-the-scenes details of running such a vast corporation and convincing billions and billions that the consumption of such an affordable treat is good for them, *Fast Food Nation* manages to visualise concepts that are, for many people, too complex or abstract to deal with on a day-to-day basis. The film is an unapologetic polemic. No facile answers are dished out and the film's irresolution is in direct contrast to the type of political films that every so often *do* make it out of Hollywood – namely the David and Goliath stories like *Norma Rae* (1979) or *Erin Brockovich* (2000): earnest yet diluted crowd pleasers that confuse outrage with social awareness.

Linklater's film does not make that mistake, which ultimately has not endeared it to many critics or audiences. They felt that the film was pedantic, oddly structured – the Greg Kinnear character, a corporate official from Mickey's who must evaluate his own personal ethics when he discovers that the restaurant chain is regularly serving up meat to customers that has feces in it, basically disappears halfway through the film – heavy-handed, and didactic. For some, the idea of sitting through a two-hour lesson in 'what you eat and where it comes from' was just too daunting, despite an intriguing (if strange) cast.

But Linklater's film does work as a piece of narrative cinema, directly recalling Godard's *Tout va bien* examination of the social dynamics of a strike at a sausage factory, as well as the earlier poetic realist short film *Le Sang des bêtes/Blood of the Beasts* (1949), directed by Georges Franju, which, like *Fast Food Nation*, concluded with graphic footage of life and death on the killing floor of the slaughterhouse. Many of the performances carry the emotional burden of the film upon their frames, giving the film's not-so-abstract though nevertheless difficult concepts a physicality. There's Kinnear as Don Anderson, the befuddled and ultimately compromised company man; Ashley Johnson as Amber, the high school student who works at Mickey's and experiences a political awakening, though, unlike Don, her moral journey is still uncluttered with pragmatic reality; and Moreno as the Mexican immigrant who crosses the border with her husband and child, and who is compromised on an economic, physical and psychological level due to her job within the slaughterhouse.

No scene better illustrates the conundrum that many people are faced with than the moment when a group of idealistic though naïve teenagers dismantle an electric fence and attempt to free the cows. Faced with the uncertainty of their newfound liberation, and the fact that, since they are bred for mass consumption, they are domesticated – i.e. paralytic – the cows do nothing. Their usefulness will come to fruition on the killing floor.

Although Hollywood is in essence an amoral, apolitical beast, outright political messages have occasionally slipped through. David O. Russell's *Three Kings* (1999) and Stephen Gaghan's *Syriana* (2005) have been two recent examples of admirable attempts to examine complex geopolitical issues within the construct of narrative filmmaking – the former within the constraints of the action film, the latter within the realm of the political thriller. Sadly, though, the extent of political thought in mainstream Hollywood fare usually goes no further than reactionary action stars wasting gormless, kill-crazy baddies (most likely in the form of a strange, multi-ethnic terrorist group with no discernable message of any kind) or earnest, socially responsible films that 'bravely' denounce racism, Nazis or Third World dictators who are determined to crush an ethnic minority until a committed though plucky journalist saves the day… or at least makes their deadline.

It's refreshing, then, that an American film as subversive as *Fast Food Nation*, with its ensemble cast, multiple storylines and ugly truths, was still able to find a seat at the marketplace dinner table. And that a director, at this stage in his career, was still hungry to make it.

DAVID O. RUSSELL

'I think that deep spiritual insight and comedy should have the same DNA.' – David O. Russell[22]

If Richard Linklater is the social conscience of this current American New Wave movement, then David O. Russell is the Holy Fool. There is a strong moral, political, and spiritual/philosophical core to Russell's work as well, something that does not really manifest itself in any of the work by Jonze, Gondry, Coppola or Anderson, but Russell's absurdist sensibility toward the world and his deftness in exposing people's pretensions without demonising them or making their plights cartoonish to the point of viewer alienation (something that director Todd Solondz *is* guilty of) does bind Russell to Jonze and the others. Like Linklater, and Soderbergh to some extent, Russell serves as a convenient and important bridge from the so-called Sundance generation of independent filmmakers to the current group, filmmakers who have maintained their ambition to make thought-provoking, narratively adventurous work that extols a certain independent spirit even though the productions are financed and released by major Hollywood studios.

Russell, more than any of the other filmmakers dealt with in this book, knows the stress and turmoil of dealing with studio bureaucrats while helming a big-budget action picture/star vehicle (*Three Kings*), something that none of the other directors in this book *wanted*, or were offered the chance to pursue. The opportunity was ostensibly a strange one for Russell to have agreed to since his two previous feature films, *Spanking the Monkey* (1994) and *Flirting with Disaster*

(1996), were continents away in both tone and subject matter from the cinematic percussion grenade that became *Three Kings*. But scratch beneath the surface of Russell's microwaved, pop-culture, Persian Gulf war film, and one of the themes from his earlier work – the inner political and spiritual transformation of an otherwise cerebrally passive or uninquisitive character into someone who is able to see the 'truth' of his own life, regardless of whether it's positive or not, and still engage with it clearly henceforth – gains a new, oddly muscular resonance. Ultimately it would also become the main theme in his last film to date, *I Heart Huckabees* (2004).

Though all of the filmmakers of this particular new wave share many of the same absurdist, comedic sensibilities and thematic preoccupations, the biggest strand that binds them together, and that separates them from the majority of their artistic peers, is that none of them attended film school. Russell, who was born and raised in New York, was an undergraduate at Amherst College in Massachusetts where he studied Political Science and English Literature before graduating in 1981. Among his teachers were acclaimed novelist Mary Gordon and Professor Robert Thurman (actress Uma Thurman's father), the leading American teacher and writer on Tibetan Buddhism.

Afterward, Russell spent some time in Nicaragua doing literacy work, and in the late 1980s and early 1990s he worked as a political activist and union organiser in Lewiston, Maine, and Boston, on community housing projects and teaching English as a second language. Those experiences, no doubt, would come in handy when he began writing *I Heart Huckabees*, basing the young, bright, earnest and neurotic environmental activist Albert Markovski loosely upon himself.

It was during that time that Russell began dabbling with making a short film, influenced by his work and friendship with members of the immigrant community in Boston that he was familiar with. The result, *Boston to Panama* (1985), is difficult to find. Russell returned to New York not long after the completion of the short film and worked a succession of low-impact jobs – working for a publisher, as a teacher, a waiter – and worked on scripts. Two more short films resulted, *Bingo*

Inferno (1987) and *Hairway to the Stars* (1990), both foregoing the more social realist take and instead incorporating and giving audiences a glimmer of the absurdist humour that would become a hallmark of Russell's subsequent formal work. *Bingo Inferno*, about an American family numbing itself to death via bingo and television, was shown at the Sundance Film Festival in 1987 and helped Russell land an NEA grant that made it possible for him to make *Hairway to the Stars*, a film focusing on an elderly woman who pays a visit to the beautician on her 50th wedding anniversary and winds up travelling through inner space while under the heat, to sometimes darkly comic effect.

Russell spent the next ten months working on a new script but to no avail, though the germ of the idea (a man seated in a Chinese restaurant spies on the customers, records their conversations with the use of tiny microphones, and then writes up personalised fortune cookie wishes) would eventually find its way back into his work with *Huckabees* in the form of the two existential detectives played by Lily Tomlin and Dustin Hoffman, obviously in a drastically revised manner.

But out of the ashes of that script's demise emerged what would eventually become Russell's feature film debut, *Spanking the Monkey*. The pitch-black chronicle of a passive young man (Jeremy Davies), his mostly bed-ridden, manipulative mother (Alberta Watson), and their rather unnatural bond was a big hit at Sundance in 1994 and ended up winning the Audience Award that year. The film also garnered two major awards at the Independent Spirit Awards, for Best First Film and Best First Screenplay, in 1995. Groomed by Miramax after the success of his first feature, Russell then made the more ambitiously delirious 'family' comedy *Flirting with Disaster* starring Ben Stiller, Patricia Arquette, Téa Leoni, Mary Tyler Moore, and Alan Alda. The psilocybin-laced, modern screwball farce was a modest hit and further displayed Russell's assured direction and handling of broad comic material without sacrificing his idiosyncratic yet perceptive depth as regards character or sly critiques of life in the great wide open of contemporary neurotic, overly medicated America. The big-budget, Operation Desert Storm war film, *Three Kings*, followed in 1999 to much critical acclaim and lukewarm box office. Five years later, Russell made what is arguably his wildest and certainly most personal film to date, *I Heart Huckabees*, a spirited, benevolently anarchic infusion of existentialist and Buddhist philosophies, wicked social satire, and a heartfelt plea for engagement with the life force of the everyday. It's the cinematic equivalent of John Lennon and Yoko Ono's 1969 Amsterdam Bed-in – a serious prank, a naïve yet vital comedic protest, and a strangely serene voice of reason and silliness that confounds as much as it inspires. Also in 2004, Russell returned to the subject of war, and the Gulf War in particular, by making a short documentary entitled *Soldiers Pay*.

It's always a satisfying jolt to watch an artist inch ever closer to the edge and somehow manage to crawl back for some convalescence before returning to the edge yet again. David O. Russell has bounded out more consistently than most and somehow always floats back to earth with perhaps more bruises and scars, but not at the expense of his boundless energy, courage, or free-flowing imagination. An increasingly difficult proposition, especially in the wake of rumours and leaked-to-the-public video evidence showing the director's sometimes volcanic temper – which has been unleashed on crew members, George Clooney and Lily Tomlin – on set. But more about that later…

Spanking the Monkey (1994)

Directed by: David O. Russell
Written by: David O. Russell
Produced by: Dean Silvers
Edited by: Pamela Martin
Cinematography by: Michael Mayers
Cast: Jeremy Davies, Benjamin Hendrickson, Alberta Watson, Carla Gallo, Matthew Puckett, Zak Orth, John Phillip Weinstein, Judah Domke, Nancy Fields, Judette Jones, Richard Husson

'All I ask is that you take care of your mother. Is that so hard?' – Tom (Benjamin Hendrickson) has no idea how wrong the answer truly is.

It seems almost unimaginable that a film about incest could be made in the United States today, but in the independent film scene of the early 1990s, film distributors and audiences alike were more open to the possibilities of something so dark and, yes, funny.

For most of us, our first introduction to writer/director David O. Russell was through viewing his startling, obsidian-black feature debut, *Spanking the Monkey*. A film so disturbing, awkward, painful, luteous, and audacious that its stains festered within the mind long after the experience was over... a griminess that lingered in some for years. When *Flirting with Disaster* was released two years later, there seemed to be a collective snap to attention and a mass whimpering that translated to, *Is this going to be more of the same*? Thankfully not. But the big question regarding *Spanking the Monkey* did persist – who in the hell was this Russell and was he really this brilliant?

Introductions are important, and Russell's was the cinematic equivalent of a damp, odious handshake. But once the off-putting salutation had faded, and the bruises of the dark comedy had abated a bit, the remarkableness of Russell's poignant, and sometimes delicately funny, coming of age/incest tale could be accurately assessed.

Incest has long been dramatic fodder for composers/musicians (Wagner, Kate Bush, Prince, The Drive-By Truckers), writers (Sophocles, John Irving, Ian McEwan, Robert Heinlein) and film (Louis Malle's *Le Souffle au coeur/Murmur of the Heart*, 1971), Bernardo Bertolucci's *La Luna* (1979) and *The Dreamers* (2003), Paul Schrader's *Cat People* remake from 1982, Gaspar Noe's *Seul contre tous/I Stand Alone* (1998) and *Borat: Cultural Learnings of America for Make Benefit Glorious Nation of Kazakhstan* from 2006, all esteemed, though unseemly, company to be sure.

But Russell's debut was much more than the sting of its potent, psychodramatically-charged metaphor. From its opening, laid-back moments on the bus when we first see the character of Raymond Aibelli (Jeremy Davies) staring out the window, daydreaming, listening to music through headphones while the sunny upstate New York countryside flashes by, Russell immediately relaxes us into what we assume will turn out to be another unassuming coming-of-age tale of the kind we've seen numerous times before. The sort of understated, naturalistic independent film crop, like Victor Nunez's *Ruby in Paradise* (1993), that Sundance audiences craved before the wake of Tarantino further demolished and redesigned the indie landscape once and for all, replacing brains and subtlety with bullets, smarminess, and hipster aloofness.

But then the old woman, played by Elizabeth Newett, offers Raymond 'another cookie' which he politely declines. She then off-handedly, though in a prickly tone of voice that only a veteran mother could project, asks him, 'What's the matter, don't you like these?' It's just the sort of stinging response that causes the viewer to pause for a moment, realising that even the most mundane exchange may come equipped with thorns. It only gets worse.

Raymond, a pre-med student on his way to his parents' home in the country for a couple of days in order to help out his mother Susan (Alberta Watson) while she convalesces from a compound fracture to her leg, is much too polite to disarm the chattering old lady with even a dismissive eyebrow. He has been raised too well to snub her increasingly irritating and irrelevant questions and asides. Raymond has manners, and, as such, is able to take punishment (even innocuous irritations like those the elderly woman dished out) with an all-American genialness that masks a horrifying, bottomless despair and repression. Raymond's foul-mouthed, hyper-tense salesman father, Tom (Benjamin Hendrickson), who appears to be working on his next heart attack, dumps on his son the shocking news that he will have to stay with his mother a lot longer than a couple of days, effectively screwing up Raymond's plans to return to Washington, D.C. for a prestigious internship with the Surgeon General. Raymond gets mad and ineffectually attempts to reason with his father, to no avail. Resigned to his perpetual role as the indecisive, weak-willed son, Raymond sees his father off at the airport and returns home to where the true test of wills plays out.

Like many of the protagonists of other films in this book, Raymond is a self-hating male character, unable to express his true feelings, desire or ambition, let alone act on any of them. He joins Adam Sandler's

Barry from *Punch-Drunk Love* (discussed later) as one of the most fragile and tortured of the bunch, though Raymond would probably also find himself quite at home with any of the male characters from Charlie Kaufman's scripts.

Over the next few days, Raymond sinks into the rituals of domesticity and subservience with deadening ease – mowing the lawn, tidying up the house, walking the dog, masturbating, or *trying* to masturbate as the case may be – as well as acting as designated caregiver, making sure his mother is comfortable in bed, mixing her afternoon drink, making her meals, emptying her bedpan, watching television with her, carrying her to the bathroom, steadying her so that she doesn't get her cast wet while she takes a shower, and so on. The house, like something out of one of Corman's Poe films from the 1960s, takes on the psychic residue of all that emotional hostility and angst. One feels suffocated within the house and the boundaries of privacy and personal space are repeatedly violated, only adding to the film's claustrophobia.

Raymond does eventually find a brief, initially innocent distraction from his purgatory when he meets a bright 17-year-old girl named Toni (Carla Gallo) who is attracted to him. But his passivity and emotional aloofness ultimately prevent him from pursuing the underage teenager, who is more mature than he is, though also more naïve. Even when the signals are clear, Raymond can't respond to her in a normal, meaningful manner – which is ultimately a good thing since Raymond is far more screwed up than she could possibly envision. When he does act on his supposed physical desires for her, something that he is goaded into after Toni asks him if he's homosexual, his detached, cold kisses and subsequent aggressive fumbling of her body is more rape than innocent summer indiscretion. Like many of the uncomfortably 'humorous' scenes in the film, the humour derives from watching a pathetic character such as Raymond dig his grave deeper and deeper into absurdity. Like most everything that he does (or doesn't do as the case may be), Raymond can't even assault Toni properly.

But however uncomfortable that scene is – and in any other film it would've been the crux of a character's downfall – the worst is yet to come. Raymond's break with the dutiful son role comes raging forth after Susan receives a call from Toni's father about the incident between Raymond and the teen. After being chastised by his mother, Susan attempts to instruct her son in how not to treat a girl and, much to our distress, how to get it done.

Russell skilfully and brazenly plunges us into Raymond and Susan's drunken transgression with the determination of a Hitchcock suspense sequence, and, like the grand master of high-concept thrills, he thrusts us into a realm of psychological quicksand that is equally claustrophobic and difficult to withstand. It's to Russell's credit, though, that we are able to keep watching. The sequence, which is handled with great fidelity, evokes a skewed tenderness and griminess that serves to plunge us further into Raymond's private hell and will ultimately serve as the catalyst for his subsequent emancipation from his family, his past, and ultimately his own cowardice. That emancipation occurs in the film's final scenes, after Raymond apparently commits suicide atop the quarry while his drunken old high school friends bicker in the dark.

Russell's film is funny in the darkest, most acidic manner, but far from the light-hearted, almost wacky tone that its marketing campaign used to lure in unsuspecting audiences. Jeremy Davies, a fascinating character actor who would go on to more prominent roles in Spielberg's *Saving Private Ryan* (1998), *CQ* (2001) and Steven Soderbergh's *Solaris* (2002), conveys the simultaneous passivity and anger that simmers within him as he stands at a crossroad in his life both professionally and personally. Raymond, like many people in their early 20s, hasn't yet learned to untether himself from his parents or his background although he longs to do so. Lured back to the family homestead, Raymond is sucked back into hanging out with old friends he no longer has anything in common with and a family life he knows is killing him. The horror – and humour – stemming from his transgression with his mother is upsetting, but only because Russell has taken the metaphor of incest so literally. It's actually not even the most destructive or damaging aspect of the situation, merely the contaminated final straw of a mother-son relationship gone bitterly venal.

Actress Alberta Watson, as Raymond's resentful and manipulative mother, also gives a brave performance, exuding just the right sort of poisonous, passive-aggressive energy and charm to lure in the unsuspecting viewer, much as she does her own son. And while Faye Dunaway was originally cast in the role (she turned it down because of the content), it's difficult to picture her in it after watching Watson's low-key, subtly anguished performance.

Made on an $180,000 budget, Russell's debut is a difficult film to warm up to. Its toxic atmosphere and abrasive low-key comedy feels unclean but, in its way, truthful. And that's where its brilliance lies. Russell redeems the unrelenting sense of true unwholesomeness in the film's final scene: within that image of the 'dead' Raymond hitch-hiking along the side of the road, we are given a moment of queasy redemption – or, at least, the possibility that such a wounded person has been given the chance to start afresh, far from the parents that have been killing him since birth.

Flirting With Disaster (1996)

Directed by: David O. Russell
Written by: David O. Russell
Produced by: Dean Silvers
Edited by: Christopher Tellefsen
Cinematography by: Eric Edwards
Cast: Ben Stiller, Patricia Arquette, Téa Leoni, Alan Alda, Mary Tyler Moore, George Segal, Lily Tomlin, Josh Brolin, Richard Jenkins, Celia Weston

'Every marriage is vulnerable, otherwise being married wouldn't mean anything, would it?' – Tina (Téa Leoni)

Unable to name his newborn son due to the fact that he doesn't yet know who his biological parents are, Mel Coplin (Ben Stiller), a neurotic New York City yuppie, receives news from the adoption case worker (Leoni) he has hired to track down his 'real' parents that his mother's name is Valerie Swaney (Celia Weston) and that she lives in San Diego. After reassuring his adoptive parents, Pearl and Ed (Mary Tyler Moore and George Segal), that he won't forsake them after his '*Roots* thing' is completed and that he just needs to reclaim his past in order to better understand who he actually is, Mel, his wife Nancy (Patricia Arquette) and Tina Kalb, the case worker (who will document the reunion for a study she is writing), head out west to meet Valerie. But Mel's search for his true identity burns out when it is awkwardly revealed that Valerie, a large-boned blonde Republican, is not Mel's mother. On the way back to New York, Mel and company journey to Detroit to meet Mel's supposed father, a rough-and-tumble ex-Hell's Angel truck driver named Fritz Boudreau (David Patrick Kelly), who 'playfully' calls his newfound son 'turd face' upon learning the news. And that's after Fritz and his buddy almost beat the hell out of Mel, Nancy and Tina. But when noticing that Mel's profile has a 'real Jew look' to it, Fritz tells him that he isn't his father either and that he only delivered baby Mel to an adoption agency back in 1965 because his mother and father were 'indisposed' at the time. After another disastrous punctuation to the disappointing news – Mel accidentally reverses Fritz's semi-truck into a post office, destroying it – and subsequent interrogation by two bickering federal agents, Tony Kent (Josh Brolin) and Paul Harmon (Richard Jenkins), the gang (including the two agents, who are actually a couple) heads down to New Mexico to seek out, hopefully once and for all, Mel's true mother and father. But when Mel finally meets his biological parents, Mary and Richard Schlichting (Lily Tomlin and Alan Alda), they are nothing like he imagined – old 60s radicals who once did some jail time for the manufacture and distribution of LSD. The reunion, strained from the start because of sexual tension and jealousy simmering between Mel, Nancy, Tina, Tony and Paul, only grows worse when the Schlichtings' troubled teenage son Lonnie (Glenn Fitzgerald), intending to spike his new brother's plate of food with some homemade acid, accidentally doses agent Paul instead. With the household in a complete uproar, especially when it's discovered that Paul is an ATF agent, Mel finally starts to gain valuable insight into what constitutes a real family and realises that perhaps one's biological parents aren't necessarily as beneficial or healthy as the family you design yourself.

The nature vs. nurture debate is deliciously turned inside out in Russell's more ambitious, star-filled-screwball comedy-inspired follow-up to *Spanking the Monkey*. And while high-concept, it transcends its sitcom plot through a steady accumulation of character detail and psychological insight. Abandoning the more unseemly family-as-torture-fest portrayed in his debut, here the proceedings, which are just as ruinous and clogged with psychological torment as their predecessor, are also more breezy and outright silly. This is pure comedy of unease. But it doesn't pummel the viewer like *Spanking the Monkey* did with its incessant, repressed, dramatic pain underlying the humour. *Flirting with Disaster* is more of a full-on volume eleven farce with claws safely filed down. The plentiful laughs, expertly timed physical gags, hyper-tense bebop dialogue and awkward tension are no more alienating than a brilliant episode of *Seinfeld*. Instead of the bitterness at the core of *Spanking the Monkey*, there is a benevolent acceptance of people's foibles, and the mistakes or biological genes of one's parents do not necessarily doom a person to a life of misery.

Though the film has its share of wonderfully uncomfortable moments, *Flirting with Disaster* hardly resembles Russell's earlier film. The neurosis and angst have not been diluted, merely assimilated thoroughly into a narrative more accommodating to fuzzy-headed gentleness and aberrant behaviour. In a way, the film retains much of the 1960s openness of mind that it parodies with the Schlichting characters – we're all freaks, but not bugs under a microscope. Perhaps Russell's unselfconscious purging and the need to literalise the most poisonous aspects of his psyche in that first film cleansed him for this more balanced appraisal of the fucked-up child within all of us. The film's colour palate, courtesy of cinematographer Eric Edwards (*My Own Private Idaho*; *Even Cowgirls Get the Blues*), gives the film a dreamy but earthy texture similar to the one that he brought to Gus Van Sant's pictures. Scenes are imbued with a warmth and glow that would have been at odds with *Spanking the Monkey*'s emotional severity, but seem right at place with this lightweight yet richly comedic offering.

Russell also gives his female leads plenty to bite into. Unlike a director such as Judd Apatow, the 'auteur' of half-baked, super-sized dude-friendly romantic comedies such as *Knocked Up* (2007), Russell isn't afraid to develop his female characters into something more than humourless housewives or vacant career women who are mere ciphers, caretakers whose sole purpose is to civilise men emerging from their protracted adolescence. In *Flirting with Disaster*, Russell offers up a range of femininity that is refreshing and in complete contrast to the fear that Raymond felt of his mother and Toni in *Spanking the Monkey*. Unlike Raymond, who must 'kill' himself at the end of the film in order to gain an opportunity at renewal, Mel simply has to accept who he is and understand that his relationship with Nancy *is* the right path, instead of throwing it all away for Tina, who in many ways is a younger version of Mel's adoptive mother, Pearl. Moore and Tomlin are a joy to watch, though the frequently miscast, comedically underutilised Patricia Arquette and Téa Leoni are superb and have rarely been better. Leoni has the sharp sexiness, intelligence and lack of vanity reminiscent of the great actresses of the screwball comedy era – Irene Dunne, Carole Lombard and Myrna Loy.

From its opening shot of an elegant, gray-haired woman striding down a Manhattan street toward the camera, while Mel narrates what his birth mother might look like, we are entering the domain of women, of the unknowable and the fear that accompanies that mystery. But when the film cuts to Patricia Arquette wearing no more than an enticement for an afternoon frolic – the fatigue of parenthood forces Mel and Nancy to pencil in 'sex dates' – the camera lovingly captures Arquette's body without lighting distortion (the scene is filmed with only the afternoon sun blazing through the curtains) or artifice of any kind. We gaze, knowing that the answer to Mel's dilemma is not as complex as he believes it is.

Flirting with Disaster was a modest hit, grossing twice its $7,000,000 budget and reviews were generally favourable. Janet Maslin, writing for the *New York Times*, hailed the film as a major step forward from his debut and noted that Russell 'now takes a huge, successful leap into wild ensemble comedy, working with a stellar cast and a remarkable number of tricks up his sleeve'.[23] Jonathan Rosenbaum, on the other hand, liked the film but found it 'a bit calculated'[24] in spite of Russell's obvious knack for comedy and Téa Leoni's performance.

Despite the success of *Flirting with Disaster*, the production of the film was tense, with persistent intervention from Miramax president (the film's production and distribution company) Harvey Weinstein, who also served as an executive producer. Notorious for his frequent re-editing of many of the films that his company acquired or for meddling in the ones that they helped make themselves, Weinstein desperately wanted to edit out a brief comedic scene at the end of the film during the credit sequence which showed the homosexual couple, played by Josh Brolin and Richard Jenkins, in bed and another shot showing the Téa Leoni character pregnant, smoking and drinking. Russell reluctantly agreed to cut the scenes, though he later reinstated them for the subsequent VHS release (they are again missing from the Region 1 DVD). Russell, disappointed and frustrated with the way he and his film were handled by Miramax, who in the mid-1990s were at the apex of their dominance in the world of independent filmmaking, would leave the roost and next journey to Hollywood, where even bigger trouble awaited him.

Three Kings (1999)

Directed by: David O. Russell
Written by: John Ridley (story); David O. Russell (screenplay)
Produced by: Paul Junger Witt, Edward L. McDonnell, Charles Roven
Edited by: Robert K. Lambert
Cinematography by: Newton Thomas Sigel
Cast: George Clooney, Mark Wahlberg, Ice Cube, Spike Jonze, Cliff Curtis, Nora Dunn, Jamie Kennedy, Saïd Taghmaoui

'I've always wanted to do an action film where a guy got a splinter.'
– David O. Russell[25]

For his next film, Russell couldn't have gotten farther from the Oedipal and Freudian preoccupations that tormented the lead characters in *Spanking the Monkey* and *Flirting with Disaster* respectively. Instead of the confines and crevasses of the neurotic, Russell expanded his horizon (and budget) by making a war film, adapting his talent for examining the internal struggles of passive characters at home to the wide open desert sands of the battlefield. But in choosing to film a story set during the 1990–91 US-led Operation Desert Storm against the then-Iraqi president/dictator Saddam Hussein, Russell was once again taking a big chance. Distancing himself from his earlier films, at least in regard to subject matter, he was now ostensibly making an 'action movie'. He was also challenging himself creatively and technically, for *Three Kings* would not be a small independent feature but a large-scale, big-budget war movie financed by a major Hollywood studio – Warner Bros. *Flirting with Disaster* may have consisted of a bigger name cast, bigger (though still modest) budget, and ultimately a bigger financial payoff than *Spanking the Monkey*, but it was still a far cry from what would be expected from Russell if he was going to take on a film set during one of the strangest and relatively underwhelming moments in modern American military history.

If Russell pulled it off, he might end up with something akin to Robert Altman's *M*A*S*H* (1970), Francis Ford Coppola's *Apocalypse Now* (1979) or Stanley Kubrick's *Full Metal Jacket* (1987). If he failed, he might find himself nestled up against Clint Eastwood's forgettable 1986 film *Heartbreak Ridge* instead, which chronicled the not-exactly-breathtaking (cinematically speaking) US invasion of Grenada in 1983.

Making *Three Kings* a successful, must-see Desert Storm film was never going to be an easy proposition in the relatively peaceful Clinton era. Previously, the only notable film to use Desert Storm as its backdrop was Edward Zwick's *Courage Under Fire* (1996) starring

Denzel Washington and Meg Ryan. Nine years after Zwick's film, and six years after Russell's production, Sam Mendes directed the film *Jarhead*, based on Anthony Swofford's visceral memoir about his time as a Marine sniper in the war. Despite Zwick's earnest and occasionally powerful morality tale and Mendes' visually arresting (courtesy of cinematographer Roger Deakins, who also lensed *Courage Under Fire*) yet politically synthetic and idea-vacant film, neither attempt resonated with audiences or captured the true mélange and clash of two cultures nose-diving into one another like Russell's film did.

Ostensibly about four US soldiers looting Kuwaiti gold bullion from one of Saddam Hussein's underground bunkers in the Iraqi desert during the final days of the US's involvement in the war, the film quickly shifts tone when the rogue soldiers witness the persecution of innocent civilians and then find themselves in a moral quagmire far from the apolitical minefields of most war films. *Three Kings* is a kinetic, highly textured mix of action, political satire, and moral fable, reminiscent of Altman's *M*A*S*H* and Mike Nichols' critically panned adaptation of Joseph Heller's modern classic absurdist anti-war novel *Catch-22*, released the same year as Altman's film. A truly subversive American war picture that also harkened back to the two-fisted World War II films like Robert Aldrich's *The Dirty Dozen* (1967) and Brian G. Hutton's *Kelly's Heroes* (1970), the latter of which found Clint Eastwood as the titular anti-hero and his ragtag band of army misfits (including Telly Savalas, Donald Sutherland and comedian Don Rickles) looting a cache of Nazi gold.

Although Russell always intended for the soldiers' plot to steal the gold to serve as a MacGuffin, the film's appropriation of generic action tropes is not merely a ploy for Russell to inundate the viewer with a two-hour humanitarian aid polemic on the evils of waging a war you cannot win. The bewildering mix of political awareness and Hollywood action filmmaking are fully integrated, and the moral choices made by Major Archie Gates (George Clooney) and his three kings (Spike Jonze, Ice Cube, Mark Wahlberg) are sophisticated, paradoxical and messy in a way that is rare for such a star vehicle.

But Russell's film is not entirely at ease with just rehashing the latter films' macho cynicism and black-hearted ironies, basically shape-shifting *Three Kings* into a frosty, bellicose 'fuck you' tailor-made for the MTV crowd. It's something that perhaps a director like David Fincher would have darkly fashioned (as he attempted for his bold though pseudo-intellectual adaptation of Chuck Palahniuk's confused and bombastic novel, *Fight Club*) or that Quentin Tarantino (as of the writing of this book) is still percolating for his long-rumoured epic World War II magnum opus, *Inglorious Bastards*. The satire may be bitter and occasionally brutal in *Three Kings*. For example, there's the opening scene in which the surrendering Iraqi soldier standing atop a faraway mound is shot by Sergeant First Class Troy Barlow (Wahlberg) when the Iraqi tilts his weapon toward Barlow only because he's confused and scared when Barlow hesitates about whether or not he's supposed to shoot or capture him (none of the other soldiers in Barlow's party seem to know either). But Russell's intent for his characters and for the audience is far more transformative and ultimately meaningful than yet another caustic, supposedly anti-war film. The scene of Barlow killing the 'raghead' does not end with our hero bragging about finally getting the opportunity to kill the enemy, but with his expression, locked in freeze frame before the opening credits flash on screen, pained and unsure after witnessing his 'kill' bleed to death. It's a jarring and unsettling opening, and a moment reminiscent of Matthew Modine's character in Stanley Kubrick's Vietnam War film, *Full Metal Jacket*, watching the Vietcong sniper bleed to death at his feet at the end of the film.

The film's crowning moment, though, occurs during the sequence when Barlow, bound to a chair, is interrogated by his Iraqi captor – superbly played by the French/Moroccan actor Saïd Taghmaoui – and then tortured. Confronting his viewers with the visceral horror of watching Barlow's torture, Russell refuses to allow the audience to feel morally superior to the Iraqi captain by giving the character the film's most startling and moving monologue of how American bombs killed his daughter. This is not mere 'political correctness' (something that Russell has *never* pandered to) but an honest and direct attempt by the filmmaker to engage us with the reality of war. Despite the jazzy infrared footage of the Baghdad bombing that was so ubiquitous at the time, images that continuously played on cable news programmes and in turn removed viewers from the direct physicality of the damage being wrought down below, Russell now has the film's 'villain' plead his case, in a manner of speaking. This, of course, doesn't condone Saïd's actions. But it does complicate the characters' moral quandaries. Like the films of Jean Renoir (and Wes Anderson), Russell's work does not contain clear villains or heroes. They are simply ordinary people trying to navigate through moral dilemmas the best that they can.

Three Kings is not a perfect film – it careens toward the melodramatic in the last act when Clooney and company deliver the Iraqis to the border – but its persistent attempt to infuse the mainstream action plot with serious moral and ethical propositions is admirable and proof that politics and real ideas *aren't* anathema to the modern-day studio picture. If anything, in a year that saw the release of some of the most provocative (if arguably overrated) American films in many a moon – *American Beauty, Fight Club, Magnolia* – *Three Kings* stood out as one of the year's best, as well as a morally coherent, visually daring and truly subversive anti-war film. The film also seems simultaneously of and ahead of its time: a surreal, disconcerting, politically aware action film that has little regard for colouring within the lines or for keeping the audience reassured when it comes to its emotional or narrative trajectory. Like the majority of films contained in this book, the writers and directors actually suppose that the people watching their films are intelligent, hungry for fresh and innovative ways of telling a story and bored by most of what comes out of Hollywood.

But at its core, as with all of Russell's films, the focus is on how characters must unleash themselves from definitions of identity, place or reality that no longer hold true in the moment. In this case, the US soldiers who are forced to rethink their usefulness once Operation Desert Storm has been abruptly 'ended', which in turn gives them the opportunity to devote all of their energies to looting the gold from the bunker. But Clooney and company aren't the only ones resistant to change. The Iraqi civilians and the Iraqi soldiers guarding the bunker have all been forced to accept the inevitable turmoil of war – the most egregious and dramatic artificial symbol of change – and their realities have shifted far more dramatically than any of the soldiers have yet experienced. This idea of individuals having to accept a new reality, be it positive or negative, is a theme that runs throughout Russell's work, from the emotional violence of *Spanking the Monkey* to *Flirting with Disaster*'s existential comedy of parenthood to *I Heart Huckabees*, which explicitly examines the spiritual and philosophical crises facing many of its characters. The world shifts, sometimes violently, and you either get it or get left behind. Underneath the sometimes flippant, go-for-the-throat style and cynicism there is serious outrage over the brutality of war and undisguised empathy for the very real people who become victims of such horror.

The collision of East and West as depicted in the film does not solely evoke images of imperialistic grandeur, of the legendary T.E. Lawrence or the fabled Babylonian kingdom of knowledge, science and poetry. Or at least, the soldiers who storm it care little for such markers or context. One of the film's most memorable images – used prominently in the trailer – is that of a Bart Simpson doll strapped on the front of a military Humvee roaring through the blisteringly hot desert. And though Russell's film felt fresh and vital when first released in 1999, the film seems even more timely in the years following the 2003 invasion and subsequent occupation of Iraq by US forces and allies.

Warner Bros. obviously thought so too. In 2004, the company arranged for the film to be re-released into theatres and onto DVD in a special edition that would include, in lieu of any extra footage not previously available, a short documentary directed by Russell, Tricia Regan and Juan Carlos Zaldívar featuring interviews with US soldiers who had served in the second Iraq war and Iraqis (including those who appeared in *Three Kings* as actors or extras) now living in the US concerning their opinions of the present war. The film, entitled *Soldiers Pay*, is a scathing and effectively balanced appraisal of the current war and the painful human cost that results from all conflict. But Warner Bros. abruptly yanked the scheduled November re-release because of time constraints, something that Russell vehemently denied, accusing the studio in turn of pulling the plug on the project because of the impending election contest between President George W. Bush and Senator John Kerry. It was a claim that the studio likewise denied. *Soldiers Pay* was eventually shown on the Independent Film Channel the evening before the 2004 election and later on DVD.

From the moment that Russell first attached himself to the project there was turmoil: from the studio who repeatedly questioned Russell's intentions on the project and whether or not he could handle such a massive production; controversy surrounding the film's original screenwriter, John Ridley, who felt betrayed that his script had been overhauled by Russell without his approval or cooperation; and the well-publicised reports that the director attacked an extra on set during the shooting of the climactic scene which subsequently erupted into a tussle with star George Clooney, who had been butting heads with the director throughout the production. Regardless of the controversy, *Three Kings* now stands as one of the great films released by a major studio in the 1990s.

I Heart Huckabees (2004)

Directed by: David O. Russell
Written by: David O. Russell, Jeff Baena
Produced by: Gregory Goodman, Scott Rudin, David O. Russell
Edited by: Robert K. Lambert
Cinematography by: Peter Deming
Cast: Jason Schwartzman, Isabelle Huppert, Dustin Hoffman, Lily Tomlin, Jude Law, Mark Wahlberg, Naomi Watts

'Have you ever transcended space and time?'
'Yes. No. Uh, time not space… No, I don't know what you're talking about.' – Existential detective Vivian Jaffee (Lily Tomlin) asks a simple question of her new client, Albert Markovski (Jason Schwartzman).

Never has the feeling of spinning out of control felt so good, so thoroughly refreshing and invigorating. To watch a filmmaker and his actors push themselves into such risky territory, dare the ridiculous and in the end manage to create something meaningful yet remain funny, is an exhilarating sight to behold. It's messy, at times (at least on a first viewing) incoherent, and consistently challenges one to relinquish one's preconceived ideas of what a commercial film – a comedy at that – can be about. And yet, somehow, it all works. It accomplishes what its director intended, which is offer up a perfectly approachable introduction to practical Zen Buddhist teachings within the constraints of an existential mystery film. A mystery though without any of the clichéd, hoary trappings of the film noir genre – detectives in trenchcoats and fedoras, overhead fans, Venetian blinds, smoke, lots of smoke, and so forth. Russell smartly steers clear of any overt film noir quotations in *Huckabees*, though with its over-baked brightness and Southern California setting – the land of fantasy and 'everyday' people, of emptiness and plenty – it evokes the sun-bleached, moral blankness of the so-called neo-noirs of the 1970s, especially Altman's 1973 revisionist *The Long Goodbye* (based on the novel by Raymond Chandler) and Roman Polanski's *Chinatown* (1974). But whereas Altman and Polanski's subversive films were hard-edged, sinister, satirical (in Altman's case) and serious in their intent to pummel the viewer with the nastiness brewing underneath the niceties of a so-called civilised society, Russell is concerned with the turmoil brewing inside each of us. If we fail to cure the malaise within, how in the hell are we expected to cure the one outside?

I Heart Huckabees is not a mystery film in a traditional sense, although the mystery at hand is literally trying to unlock the Human Condition. It's a sweet, surreal comedy, chock full of post-9/11 anxiety, and perhaps the most audacious, imaginative and original American film since Charlie Kaufman and Spike Jonze arrived on the film scene with *Being John Malkovich* in 1999. There is a real spirit of experimentation infused throughout its script (written by Russell and Jeff Baena), a warped yet completely realised and methodical display of playfulness with serious intent.

Ostensibly about the plight of environmental activist and head of the Open Spaces Coalition, Albert Markovski (Jason Schwartzman), as he attempts to save an urban wildlife area from greedy land developers (are there any other kind?), Albert's quixotic struggle against the forces of commerce is seemingly thwarted when the coalition's crusade is compromised by its involvement with the Huckabees Corporation (the company that owns a chain of department stores), specifically its demonically ambitious young executive Brad Stand (Jude Law). Brad's facile charm – he repeatedly tells an unfunny anecdote about singer Shania Twain and a tuna fish sandwich to anyone who will listen, which is most anyone, unfortunately – wins everyone over, except Albert, who becomes increasingly hostile to his new sponsor when he suspects that Brad is successfully trying to gain lordship over Open Spaces. Feeling that his own involvement in the grassroots organisation is being undermined by the self-serving Brad, Albert spins out of control with negative and destructive thoughts. But due to a moment of supreme serendipity, Albert enlists the help of Jaffee & Jaffee, Existential Detectives, a husband-and-wife team – Bernard (Dustin Hoffman) and Vivian (Lily Tomlin) – who agree to help the angst-filled, jealousy-plagued conservationist get to the crux of his cosmic/mundane situational confusion. But things are complicated even more when a former protégé and rival of the Jaffees enters the picture, Caterine Vauban (Isabelle Huppert). Caterine eventually seduces Albert with her harsh Nietzschean/nihilistic philosophy (her business card reads: 'Cruelty, Manipulation, Meaninglessness'), showing him a viable, albeit more brutal alternative to the Jaffees' more transcendentalist approach to finding one's place within the universe.

Similar to Russell's strip-mining of genre clichés in *Three Kings*, with his fourth film, *I Heart Huckabees*, Russell and co-writer Baena subverted the conventions of the traditional hard-boiled mystery novel in the Hammett/Chandler mould, by casting its young environmentalist activist hero into a major crisis of personal identity while simultaneously becoming both investigator and subject. The film's script, which oscillates between over-the-top silliness, profound yet simple insights, vicious, clear-eyed satire and bruising truths – sometimes at the same time! – frequently feels like it's losing control. But somehow the film doesn't implode. Somehow the layers of meaning cascade over the stretched-out satire without distorting the whole, without creating the pretentious disaster that it could have easily become. Although the script is one of the most original (and funny) of recent vintage and contains a steady stream of lightning-fast one-liners and cerebral non sequiturs, the film's greatest strength is the range of pitch-perfect performances from the entire ensemble, especially actor Mark Wahlberg as Tommy Corn, a seriously stressed-out firefighter whose marriage as well as his mental health is falling apart in the wake of his newfound crusade against all petroleum products because of their detrimental effect on the environment. Jude Law and Naomi Watts (as the 'face' of Huckabees and Brad's girlfriend) also turn in superbly grotesque performances, admirably lampooning their own superstar images.

At times uncomfortable, flaky, brilliant, vicious in its satire yet forgiving in its appraisal of faults found, insightful in its dissemination of a variety of personality types, and just plain wickedly funny as it explores life in America post-9/11 – with all its rigidity, obsession over body type, rampant consumerism and absurdity intact – Russell and company have crafted the strangest film to come off the Hollywood production line in recent memory, recalling a time when the studios let escape true anarchic curiosities such as Theodore J. Flicker's *The President's Analyst* (1967) starring James Coburn or Otto Preminger's all-star LSD comedy *Skidoo* (1968), which featured Jackie Gleason, Carol Channing, Groucho Marx and many others, turning on, dropping out, and discovering that audiences and critics aren't always kind to the cinematic equivalent of a natural oddity.

Unfortunately, the film failed to capture much of an audience when it was released by Fox Searchlight Pictures in the fall of 2004 – making a little over half of its $22,000,000 budget – and not surprisingly split the critics into love-it-or-hate-it camps. David Denby, writing for the *New Yorker*, lambasted the film for its chaotic comedic power and seemed genuinely perplexed by Russell's seriousness in asking philosophical questions despite the film's more manic qualities, ultimately branding it an 'authentic disaster'.[26] Andrew Sarris, on the other hand, found the film's lack of a traditional narrative structure commendable and, despite its excessive stylisation, pronounced *Huckabees*' charms both 'sweet and buoyant',[27] subsequently putting the film on his best of the year list. Since its release, the film has gone on to accumulate a fervent fan base, as well as generating some controversy along the way.

Russell's reputation as a provocateur is not solely relegated to what winds up on the screen. His sets can be just as volatile and Russell's need to work fluidly and in an improvisatory manner is difficult for some actors to deal with, as George Clooney discovered during the production of *Three Kings*. *I Heart Huckabees* was no different, though this time evidence of the abrasiveness unleashed on the set was leaked to the public. In the spring of 2007 two videos reared their ugly heads, the first one showing the director and star Lily Tomlin erupting into obscenity-laden tirades when Tomlin professes that she no longer understands what Russell wants from her. Although the fight is shocking in its abusive onslaught and because of Russell's intimidating loss of control, there is a huge element of humour in the proceedings as well, as actor Jason Schwartzman calmly sits within the middle of the maelstrom and Dustin Hoffman quietly scuttles off the set, no doubt to a calmer corner of the studio. The second video features stars Tomlin, Hoffman and Isabelle Huppert in the front seat of a parked car and Mark Wahlberg and Naomi Watts in the back seat, out of frame but clearly heard. Tomlin, again the focus of the meltdown, loses her cool and proceeds to berate the director, the production and her fellow actors. The footage is nothing more than an embarrassing footnote in the careers of Russell and Tomlin, mentioned here because it illuminates the free associative, improvisatory nature that gives Russell's films a distinctive personality separate from others. It also highlights the pressures that are a regular part of any major studio production and how a filmmaker such as Russell, someone who feeds off of spontaneity, does not always react to the high-pressure environment in a civilised manner. Tomlin and Russell are not the first people to have meltdowns on a set due to the pressure of hopefully creating something unique. But they may be the first to have their antics available for the whole world to gape over.

It will be interesting to see where a true deviant like Russell goes after *I Heart Huckabees*, his most personal film to date and one that succeeds despite its neurotic energy in finding an oasis of calm and thoughtfulness amongst the darkness and stress of modern life. Although Russell no doubt will continue to beguile audiences in the future, it's tempting to see this as his skewed masterpiece. Not simply because the film solidifies his position as a true practitioner within the screwball comedy genre (even while he reconfigures the conventions of the genre for modern audiences), but because he managed to create one of the most genially thought-provoking yet subversive mainstream films from a major studio ever.

WES ANDERSON

'Watch this space. What does that mean? That he might be something one day.' – David Thomson on Wes Anderson[28]

Three sentences. Fifteen syllables. But that's all it took to land such a
dismissive backhanded compliment to one of the most peculiar original voices and visual senses in cinema today. Critic and writer David
Thomson, though, isn't the only one disappointed with the trajectory
of Anderson's career after the praise heaped upon his first two films.

On the other hand, in a 2000 article in *Esquire*[29] magazine, one of
America's most respected living filmmakers, Martin Scorsese, was a
bit more laudatory when asked who would be the next... him. On the
strength of Anderson's debut feature, *Bottle Rocket* (1996), a spry re-
evaluation of the moribund post-Tarantino heist pictures that had been
clogging up theatres and video-store shelves ever since the release
of *Reservoir Dogs* in 1991, and the magnificent, completely assured
sophomore juggernaut *Rushmore* (1998), the great Scorsese selected
Anderson as the heir to his celluloid throne.

And why not? Anderson, unlike, say, Tim Burton – another meticulous visual stylist – is not a hollow miniaturist, a glorified model-maker
unfortunately saddled with a gaggle of actors to deal with. All of Anderson's films are in love with actors and dialogue, as well as steeped
in a conscious appreciation of the relevance of literature, music, paint-
ing, and cinema, as they relate to their human counterparts and shape
their realities. It's a strong trait that he shares with his *nouvelle vague*
progenitors, especially Truffaut, whose strong love of literature often

found representation in his films. Anderson's assimilation of literature into his films, much like his incorporation of theatrical techniques and visual motifs such as mannered framing, theatrical opening credit sequences, use of title cards or chapter headings to denote a segue into a new act, the 'final bow' given to his cast of characters ('a good cast is worth repeating'), is always cinematic, always meant to lend the films an added layer of aesthetic dialecticism that does not exist outside of the frame per se. Anderson's penchant for artifice is also what so many of his detractors seem to dislike about his films – the recurring motifs, the self-conscious framing, immaculately tailored mix-tape song lists that time and again include music from the 1960s British Invasion, and the wilful desire to encase his characters within what they argue is an increasingly rarefied bubble of whimsy and twee that has started to resemble, with each successive movie, something synthetic, something less about us and more and more about *stuff*.

In the eyes of his critics, and even his most ardent fans, who feel that this extraordinary talent has simply become much too enamoured of the glimmering cinematic train set at his disposal, Anderson is a brilliant technician who has lost his way along the road to greatness. Whereas the precocious talent from Texas first slipped snugly inside Truffaut's shoes, Anderson now appears to have gravitated more toward the exaggerated arrangements and eccentric notes of a post-*Giulietta degli spiriti/Juliet of the Spirits* (1965) Fellini, a time when the maestro of Italian cinema stretched his already strong predilection for surrealism, extravagance, and amplified caricature into hyperdrive with his subsequent work, *Fellini Satyricon* (1969), *Fellini's Roma* (1972), and, at his most hyperbolic, fascinating and ultimately exhausting, the failed *Il Casanova di Federico Fellini* (1976).

It's unknown whether or not Wes Anderson will, or should, heed the pleas to 'return to form' from his most obsessed and disappointed fans. It's sort of like requesting that David Lynch stop being so weird. Anderson, with his collection of moneyed misfits, broken sons searching for authoritarian yet comforting father figures, need for unity and acceptance within a family unit (traditional or of one's making), and a surprisingly earnest and heartfelt emotional core that has infused *all* of his films – including the much maligned and misunderstood *Life Aquatic with Steve Zissou* – has been one of the most consistent and coherent cinematic voices of his generation. His themes, namely those of brotherhood, friendship, fallen-from-grace prodigies and eccentrics searching for redemption, may for some be a limited colour palette to choose from, but it's no different from that of directors like Ford, Hitchcock, Kubrick, Scorsese, and the previously mentioned Lynch, who extracted great insight and meaning out of their own rich and somewhat restricted themes or through repetitive stylistic signatures. But growth is also part of an artist's worth, and, for many, Anderson has simply not displayed any desire to move beyond the corridors of the familiar.

Anderson was born in 1969 in Houston, Texas to an upper-middle-class family, a background that would provide a rich texture for all of his films – class differences being a major theme throughout, though typically addressed in an off-hand, low-key manner. Many of Anderson's protagonists are either part of the upper middle class or want to belong to it. But despite their privilege, few of them, if any, are actually happy, whether it's Anthony (Luke Wilson) in *Bottle Rocket*, who at the beginning of the film has just left a mental hospital that he admitted himself to, or the entire burned-out Tenenbaum clan of well-off dreamers and depressives who seem desperate to escape the confinements of a tarnished prerogative. Suspended in their privilege and perpetual adolescence, the key to self-awareness only arrives with tragedy, i.e. the death of a close friend or family member.

After spending his teens attending St. John's School in Houston, where he later filmed much of *Rushmore*, and where, like that film's precocious playwright extraordinaire Max Fischer (Jason Schwartzman), he staged elaborate theatrical productions like *The Battle of the Alamo* and *The Headless Horseman*,[30] Anderson enrolled at the University of Texas in Austin where he majored in philosophy. It was there that he eventually met Owen Wilson, who was majoring in creative writing, in a playwriting class. Although the two were in the same class, they never actually spoke to one another until their second semester, but they quickly became fast friends once they realised that they shared similar tastes in literature and film. The culmination of their late-night discussions of filmmaking led to brainstorming screenplay ideas, and it was then that the two precocious, budding filmmakers started working on what would ultimately become the short black-and-white film *Bottle Rocket*.

Wilson's family was friends with L.M. Kit Carson, the actor/writer who had previously starred in Jim McBride's classic experimental *nouvelle vague*-influenced *David Holzman's Diary* (1967) and gone on to script McBride's *Breathless* (1983) remake and also Wim Wenders' *Paris, Texas* (1984). Carson became interested in the project and invited both Anderson and Wilson to accompany him and his wife Cynthia Hargrave to the 1992 Sundance Film Festival. McBride and Hargrave would both serve as *Bottle Rocket*'s producers. Journeying to Sundance that year was an eye-opening experience for the two novices, and luckily they found investors to film the short. Upon completion of the 13-minute film, Anderson and Wilson returned to Sundance hoping to drum up investors for a full-length feature version. Reaction to the film was strong at the annual independent film festival but no offers trickled down their way.

But interest in Hollywood for a feature-length version of the peculiar, skewed take on the heist genre did manifest itself in the shape of the multi-talented Polly Platt, ex-wife and artistic collaborator of director Peter Bogdanovich. Platt, who fell in love with the script's clever but down-home humour, eccentric, naïve characters and genuine tenderness embedded within what is, in actuality, a ridiculous plot, passed the script on to James L. Brooks, who, with Platt, would become *Bottle Rocket*'s guiding light and producer.

Bottle Rocket, the feature film, was released by Columbia Pictures in 1996 and would garner strong critical praise. But the studio dumped the film and it would only be through video and DVD that this American comedic gem, one of the true stand-out independent features of the 1990s, would find its audience.

Despite the commercial failure of his debut, Anderson's future was bright and for his next film his ambition as a filmmaker was broader and more adventurous. *Rushmore* starred then-unknown Jason Schwartzman as the precociously brilliant playwright/inventor/renaissance teen Max Fischer, a student at the titular private school who vies with his friend, a downwardly mobile, married, middle-aged steel tycoon, played by Bill Murray, for the love of a beautiful new teacher at the school. Audacious and completely fresh, while still paying homage to a wealth of cinematic influences ranging from Mike Nichols' *The Graduate* to Louis Malle's *Le Souffle au coeur* to Hal Ashby's *Harold and Maude* (1971) to the films of John Hughes (*Sixteen Candles*, *Ferris Bueller's Day Off*), Anderson's second film was a wonderful and unique reimagining of the teen comedy genre and a far cry from the frat boy, gross-out *Porky*'s throwback of *American Pie* that would rear up and dominate the box office a year later.

In 2002, Anderson released the exquisitely designed, hyper-realistic fairy tale of a New York that never was, *The Royal Tenenbaums*, starring a first-rate ensemble cast headed by Gene Hackman, Anjelica Huston, Gwyneth Paltrow, Ben Stiller, and Luke and Owen Wilson. Sprawling yet intimate, the film unfurls like a peculiar masterpiece of some kind, perfectly balancing Anderson's painterly attention to the clear-lined *mise-en-scène* while delivering sometimes devastating emotional blows. The film would become Anderson's most celebrated work up to that point, earning praises from both fans and critics. But its ambitious visual scope and leanings toward a more formal – though some would argue a more solipsistic, self-conscious or precious – hermetic design, would also lay the groundwork for what many critics saw as a major artistic stumble.

That setback, for many, would come in the form of his next picture, *The Life Aquatic with Steve Zissou*. Part parody/tribute to the late, great French sea explorer Jacques Cousteau, part surreal though user-friendly peculiarity as remixed by Walt Disney, *Life Aquatic* is a phantasmagoric, big-budget love letter to the legendary Cousteau, Rome's famed Cinecittà film studios (where much of it was filmed) and to his lead actor, Bill Murray. Murray played the embittered oceanographer Steve Zissou, whose best days have long passed him by – an Anderson preoccupation – but who is determined to track down the mythical jaguar shark that killed his friend and comrade, Esteban. Fitted with his biggest studio budget yet and access to all of the toys any filmmaker would love to have at their disposal while filming at Cinecittà, Anderson indulged his odd imagination like never before. But *Life Aquatic* – like many of his films – generated mixed reviews, tepid box office, and reinforced the view held by many of his fans that the absence of Wilson's participation on the script was detrimental to the film. Regardless of the perceived artistic inadequacies of the film, the negative reviews, or the dissatisfying box office, *Life Aquatic* has its fair share of defenders, this author being one of them.

In between productions, Anderson has directed several commercials promoting everything from Dasani water to AVON to IKEA furniture. But his most widely seen promo was for American Express, in which the director played himself 'on the set' of his latest picture, an action epic starring Jason Schwartzman among others, and that precisely paid homage to François Truffaut's classic 1973 film about the making of a film, *La nuit Americaine/Day for Night*. The ad condensed much of Anderson's visual template with its sumptuously composed frames and fluid camerawork, courtesy of cinematographer Robert Yeoman. Whether people in their living rooms realised it or not, they had just watched a two-minute masterstroke by the most overly praised yet undervalued American filmmaker working today.

In September of 2007, Wes Anderson's long-awaited follow-up to *Life Aquatic*, *The Darjeeling Limited* (along with the 13-minute short film, *Hotel Chevalier*, starring Natalie Portman and Jason Schwartzman and described as 'a short epilogue of one heartbreaking history of love', which serves as a prologue to the events in the feature film), was unveiled at the 64th Venice Film Festival. Typically, critical reactions to the picaresque sojourn of three brothers riding the rails through rural India – the dreamland of Kipling and Satyajit Ray – after the death of their father, ranged from the hostile[31] to the adoring.[32]

Bottle Rocket (1996)

Directed by: Wes Anderson
Written by: Owen Wilson, Wes Anderson
Produced by: Cynthia Hargrave, Polly Platt
Edited by: David Moritz
Cinematography by: Robert Yeoman
Cast: Luke Wilson, Owen Wilson, James Caan, Robert Musgrave, Andrew Wilson, Lumi Cavazos

'One morning, over at Elizabeth's beach house, she asked me if I'd rather go water-skiing or lay out. And I realised that not only did I not want to answer *that* question, but I never wanted to answer another water-sports question, or see any of these people again for the rest of my life.' – Anthony (Luke Wilson) explaining why he was hospitalised for 'exhaustion'.

Peter Pans, men who never willingly grow up until circumstances force them out of their prolonged adolescence, figure strongly in all of Wes Anderson's films, though perhaps never as amicably or as pronouncedly as in his debut feature, *Bottle Rocket*. Although the fate of one character, Dignan (Owen Wilson), lands a quiet emotional blow at the finale, which resonates like a devastating whisper long after the film has ended, the push toward maturity for the three aspiring, bumbling criminals – Anthony (Luke Wilson), Bob (Robert Musgrave), and Dignan – has up to that point been played for comedy, albeit of the wistful sort. These three well-off, upper-middle-class suburban youths, who are determined to live life under the radar but not necessarily on the cheap, would be portrayed by any other director – say, Kevin Smith – as the sad-sack louts that they are, losers of the first order. They're certainly charming, though, no doubt courtesy of the engaging performances from Luke and Owen, who have rarely been better, and the exquisitely laconic Robert Musgrave as the gang's wheel man, who still lives at home with his parents and his knuckle-dragging brother, Future Man (Andrew Wilson), and who looks like he'd rather just be tending to the pot plants he keeps hidden in the backyard or lounging on the couch sipping a vodka tonic than committing hard crimes.

Yet these 'losers' are anything but, really. Focused and certainly ambitious, Anthony, Dignan and Bob are hardly unmotivated moochers, pessimistic hustlers forever trying to remain stationary (their habitat the couch) and preferably in their parents' basement. Upon Anthony's release from the mental health clinic, Dignan earnestly presents him with a 75-year-long plan for how their lives should progress, much like a child would devise. It's a significant detail, and indicative of Anderson and Wilson's sympathy toward their characters. Dignan is not the easiest character to like; in fact, his controlling, self-absorbed delusions of petty grandeur make it easier to dismiss him as just another loony. But his belief in the value and honour of camaraderie, of devotion to a cause, and his never-say-die attitude – his refusal to give in to cynicism, something that his friend Anthony also shares, though not Bob – make it difficult to dismiss him so readily. Even when it's apparent that Dignan is making the wrong move – and that occurs more than a few times throughout the film – it's hard not to feel something for this hopelessly romantic towhead with a buzz cut, who should be riding side-kick to John Wayne in a parallel universe version of *Rio Bravo* (1959). Instead, Dignan is trapped, lost somewhere in the suburbs of America. But no way is he going to let that get him down, no sir. He's going to make the best of it. Even when he is confronted with the harsh reality of spending the next few years behind bars, you know he'll make it somehow. Nevertheless, the final image of Dignan trying to keep up appearances behind bars while his friends depart is haunting, a moment of true brilliance and wisdom in a film that had already earned its place as one of the best American films of the 1990s.

When it was released in 1996, *Bottle Rocket* was a breath of fresh air for an increasingly jaded indie-film crowd. As scripted by Anderson and actor Owen Wilson, the film's soft-heeled Texas charm and unassuming performances offered up an array of deadpan eccentricity and over-caffeinated oddness. But somehow the film never stretched too far into the broad comedy and cartoonishness that typified so many

American comedies at the time, from that served up by indie darlings the Coen Brothers to the more mainstream Farrelly Brothers, and that would increasingly seep into Anderson's own subsequent work. There was a genuine fragile humanity and tenderness at hand in *Bottle Rocket*, as well as a real sense that a fresh and perhaps vital new voice was indeed ready to balance the scales a bit after the onslaught of post-Tarantino genre genuflections. The film was an unabashed antidote to saccharine tearjerkers like Nora Ephron's *Sleepless in Seattle* (1993) and the Farrelly Brothers' half-wit slapstick film *Dumb and Dumber* (1994) that dominated screens at the time. *Bottle Rocket*, as with *Spanking the Monkey*, was a modest appeal for comedic filmmakers to return to the possibilities that Mike Nichols and Hal Ashby had set forth 20 years earlier.

Anderson's first film would inaugurate plenty of long-lasting working relationships besides that with the ubiquitous Wilson brothers. Cinematographer Robert Yeoman, who got his start working second unit on William Friedkin's underrated neo-noir *To Live and Die in LA* (1985) – taking over main duties when the film's main cinematographer Robbie Muller, Wim Wenders' longtime collaborator, had to leave the production – would later go on to contribute greatly to Gus Van Sant's gritty yet lyrical *Drugstore Cowboy* (1989). His work for *Bottle Rocket* would display a similarly exaggerated naturalism with its deceptively simple framing and by showing us locations that are obvious and unique at the same time. Like his mentor Robbie Muller, Yeoman has a knack for engaging us with the parts of environments that we are all familiar with but rarely pay attention to – suburban back alleys, a field behind a motel, parking lots, warehouses. For subsequent films with Anderson, Yeoman's style would move away from the naturalistic – as Anderson's films have – and his framing would become more intricate, formal and rigid.

Part stunted coming-of-age tale, part abbreviated road picture, part love story that simultaneously felt like a wrong turn and the sweetest detour worth your attention, and part absurdist heist picture of the kind the Marx Brothers might have favoured, *Bottle Rocket* was one of the most satisfying and unexpected delights of 1996. Besides introducing to the world the Wilson brothers, Anderson also reintroduced to a new generation the swaggering charm of actor James Caan – whose long, up-and-down career had been mostly down throughout the 1980s and 90s despite some quality, noticeable work in films like Francis Ford Coppola's *Gardens of Stone* (1987), *Misery* (1990) and *Flesh and Bone* (1993). It's a fine, growly performance and a small taste of the accomplished performances Anderson would get from veteran male actors in the years to come.

Rushmore (1998)

Directed by: Wes Anderson
Written by: Wes Anderson, Owen Wilson
Produced by: Barry Mendel, Paul Schiff
Edited by: David Moritz
Cinematography by: Robert Yeoman
Cast: Jason Schwartzman, Bill Murray, Olivia Williams, Seymour Cassel, Brian Cox, Mason Gamble, Sara Tanaka, Stephen McCole, Connie Nielsen, Luke Wilson

'What's the secret, Max?' – Bill Murray in *Rushmore*

It's a simple question… and one entirely mystifying. Resourceful, diligent, feverishly optimistic, Max Fischer (Jason Schwartzman), the proverbial teenage Jack-of-all-trades hero of Wes Anderson's second film, *Rushmore*, is the type of protagonist that makes an impression whether you're ready for him or not. The sort of irrepressible, suspicious, fearless, self-made American scalawag that has infiltrated literature in the guise of Twain's Huck Finn and Salinger's Holden Caulfield, and film with the likes of Dustin Hoffman's Benjamin Braddock in Mike Nichols' *The Graduate* (1967), Bud Cort's death-obsessed prankster Harold in Hal Ashby's *Harold and Maude* and Matthew Broderick's eponymous suburban slacker in *Ferris Bueller's Day Off* (1986). Fischer's antecedents, of course, shouldn't be limited to simply American rebels, especially when characters such as the young ruffian Antoine Doinel (Jean-Pierre Léaud), from Truffaut's *Les Quatre cents coups*, and the public school subversive/radical Mick (Malcolm McDowell) in Lindsay Anderson's Brit New Wave Molotov cocktail, *if....* (1968), among others, are equally responsible for informing, shaping, and encouraging such a troublemaker as Max in his quest for victory over the timid establishment. Every generation needs its fictional cultural terrorists, be it an Alex DeLarge or a Bugs Bunny. Max, fortunately, contains a little bit of both to satiate fans of both extremes.

Enrolled at the prestigious academy of Rushmore, Max Fischer (who gained entry into the private school through a scholarship) bobs and weaves through his schooling with arguably more enthusiasm and determination to make things creative (he's the head of or belongs to numerous extracurricular clubs such as the debating club, the French club, the beekeeping club, the gun club, the chess club) than an aptitude for structured education. Max is also a habitual liar – his father, played by Seymour Cassel, is a barber, though Max tells everyone at school that he is a neurosurgeon – and an awful student. 'He's one of the worst,' as Rushmore's headmaster Dr Guggenheim (Brian Cox) glumly informs an inquisitive Herman Blume (Bill Murray), a Vietnam War vet and local steel tycoon, after he meets the boy and his faithful companion, Dirk (Mason Gamble), for the first time. Blume, a self-made man from a working-class background, has just delivered a speech to the academy emphasising the need for the privileged students to question their position within the society and to 'take down' the more fortunate. To no one's surprise, the speech falls flat except for Max's lone standing ovation.

Max and Blume's bond, their shared antipathy toward the so-called establishment, will inform their friendship. The middle-aged Blume, who is depressed and no longer identifies with the man that he has become (it's as if we are peering into the disconnected middle years of Dustin Hoffman's character from *The Graduate*, perhaps the most significant and meaningful influence on *Rushmore*, after the bloom of romance has tempered and the malaise of marriage has been inculcated upon yet another unwary victim), sees in Max what he once was or aspired to be. Max does very much the same; his lack of first-hand life experience leaves him unprepared for the inevitability of the cracks that form as a result of living a compromised life. It's a realisation that has come to Blume almost too late.

Their friendship is nevertheless complicated when Max meets a new first grade teacher at the school, Rosemary Cross (Olivia Williams), an English widow whose husband used to attend the academy. Max is immediately amorous toward Miss Cross. And though she is fond of Max, Miss Cross's intentions with the far younger pupil are strictly within the realm of the platonic. But Max refuses to back down, and he launches a series of attempts to woo Miss Cross, including convincing Blume to finance the building of a gigantic aquarium at the school, a feat that subsequently gets Max expelled. Blume likewise falls in love with Miss Cross and behind Max's back carries on a clandestine relationship with her. That is until Max is tipped off and wages a savage (and savagely funny) war of attrition upon his dear friend, proving that love indeed inflicts strange wisdom upon men.

Synopsising *Rushmore*'s plot is simple enough, but it doesn't come close to detailing the film's marvellous nuances, its carefully orchestrated style, or the extraordinary performances from its leading players and peripheral supporting cast. What's also immediately apparent from Anderson's sophomore effort is its complete fluidity and assurance in its own snow-globe portrayal of its environment – here is a world completely real though slightly exaggerated; the first true glimpse of what this completely unique director/writer will deliver in films to come, from the fantasised New York of *The Royal Tenenbaums* to the sweeping brown vistas of India that form the setting for the searching, grieving brothers of *The Darjeeling Limited*. But here, amidst the ivy-covered sanctuary of the Rushmore academy, populated with a thoroughly realised assortment of exaggerated characters, Anderson and co-screenwriter Owen Wilson unveil a tour de force of comedic peculiarity and unapologetic emotion. Arch and mannered though his films may be on a stylistic level, they are nevertheless warm, deeply

Before Sunrise (1995). Dir. Richard Linklater. Shown: Julie Delpy (as Céline), Ethan Hawke (as Jesse). Castle Rock Entertainment/Photofest. © Castle Rock Entertainment

The Royal Tenenbaums (2001). Dir. Wes Anderson. Shown from left: Luke Wilson
(as Eli Cash), Gwyneth Paltrow (as Margot Tenenbaum).
Touchstone Pictures/Photofest. ©Touchstone Pictures

The Life Aquatic with Steve Zissou (2004). Dir. Wes Anderson. Shown: Director Wes Anderson, behind the wheel of a submersible specially designed for the film. Touchstone Pictures/Photofest. © Touchstone Pictures

The Darjeeling Limited (2007). Dir. Wes Anderson. Shown from left: Owen Wilson (as Francis Whitman), Jason Schwartzman (as Jack Whitman), Adrien Brody (as Peter Whitman). © Fox Searchlight

I Heart Huckabees (2004). Dir. David O. Russell. Shown: Jason Schwartzman (as Albert Markovski), Jude Law (as Brad Stand). Fox Searchlight/Photofest. © Fox

Adaptation (2002). Dir. Spike Jonze. Shown: Nicolas Cage as Charlie Kaufman ("Story"), Nicolas Cage as Donald Kaufman. Columbia Pictures/Photofest. © Columbia Pictures

Eternal Sunshine of the Spotless Mind (2004). Dir. Michel Gondry.
Shown: Kate Winslet, Jim Carrey. Focus Features/Photofest. © Focus Features

Lost in Translation (2003). Dir. Sofia Coppola. Scarlett Johansson (as Charlotte),
Bill Murray (as Bob Harris). Focus Features/Photofest. © Focus Features

Marie Antoinette (2006). Dir. Sofia Coppola. Shown: Kirsten Dunst.
Sony Pictures Entertainment/Photofest. © Sony Pictures Entertainment
Photographer: Leigh Johnson

CQ (2001). Dir. Roman Coppola. Shown: Angela Lindvall. United Artists/Photofest.
© United Artists

Donnie Darko (2001). Dir. Richard Kelly. Shown: Jake Gyllenhaal (as Donnie Darko). Pandora Cinema/Photofest. © Pandora Cinema

affectionate toward the oddball characters that populate them, and generously inclusive toward the audience without pandering to them. And at a moment in time when the American independent film scene was offering up brutal ironists like Todd Solondz (*Happiness*) – Anderson's antithesis if ever there was one – Rushmore's affable knuckleheads were a welcome surprise.

With *Rushmore*, Anderson completely bypassed the sophomore slump. And though it was saddled with a low budget ($20,000,000) for a film financed by Disney (Touchstone Pictures), it was a significant step up from the independently financed *Bottle Rocket*. With his second film, Anderson was able to unleash his imagination a bit more, refashioning his hometown of Houston, Texas (where the film was shot) into the sort of slightly broad, naturalistic textures that he would fine-tune over time and infuse with more and more layers of painterly detail. But here, the 'excess' that would – for many – taint Anderson's subsequent work was still in check, still light enough not to distract from the all-too-human comedy on display.

The Royal Tenenbaums (2001)

Directed by: Wes Anderson
Written by: Wes Anderson, Owen Wilson
Produced by: Wes Anderson, Barry Mendel, Scott Rudin
Edited by: Dylan Tichenor
Cinematography: Robert Yeoman
Cast: Danny Glover, Gene Hackman, Anjelica Huston, Bill Murray, Gwyneth Paltrow, Ben Stiller, Luke Wilson, Owen Wilson

'I'm not talking about dance lessons. I'm talking about putting a brick through the other guy's windshield. I'm talking about taking it out and chopping it up.' – Royal Tenenbaum (Gene Hackman) speaking with his estranged wife Etheline (Anjelica Huston) about the right way to raise his grandsons.

Failure, despair and death are not usually the themes of a great comedy, but with *The Royal Tenenbaums* Wes Anderson filled his ambitious, almost epic (for him) chronicle of a fractured, not-so-normal, American family with just those elements. And for all its focus on misfortune and disillusionment, the film *is* a comedy, although one that feels like heartbreak.

It begins in a mad dash. A whirling dervish of a prologue whips us through the rise and fall of the once mighty, eccentric Tenenbaum clan – the patriarch Royal (Hackman), his archeologist and writer wife Etheline (Huston), the tennis pro Richie (Luke Wilson), financial wizard and entrepreneur Chas (Ben Stiller) and playwright Margot (Gwyneth Paltrow), who is also adopted – riffing off of Truffaut's own breathtaking opening to *Jules et Jim*. But as with *Rushmore*, Anderson is not really interested in examining the prototypical American fascination with triumph. He's interested in the burnout, the stasis of failure that plagues once promising talent. As J.D. Salinger's great American novel of youth rebellion, *The Catcher in the Rye*, is to *Rushmore*, Salinger's Glass Family stories are to *The Royal Tenenbaums*, an exquisitely rendered comedy of ill-manners, depression and life in the shadow of one's reputation.

The blur of the prologue (narrated in perfect deadpan fashion by actor Alec Baldwin) is spatially and temporally liberating as it sprints through the family's rise and fall. But afterwards, when the real story begins, the pace settles for us to behold and feel the malaise that has laid waste to these crippled overachievers. With the sparkle of success they were viewed affectionately as eccentrics. Now, older and festering with disappointment, they're misfits and losers – *Peanuts* characters on the skids. The Charles Schulz reference is a pertinent one, since Anderson frequently honours the creator of Charlie Brown (the funny papers' greatest blockhead of them all) with sly nods – making Max Fischer's father in *Rushmore* a barber, like Schulz's own father, using Vince Guaraldi's music in the original *Bottle Rocket* short and in *The Royal Tenenbaums*.

Richie, with his Bjorn Bjorg-style headband, shades and beard, no longer plays tennis after suffering an inexplicable breakdown during a tournament. He now wanders the sea on an ocean liner. Margot no longer writes. Now married to an older man named Raleigh St. Clair (Bill Murray), a famous neurologist, she spends most of her time in the bathroom chain-smoking and hiding the fact from everyone. Businessman Chas is fighting to keep it all together as he grapples with the pain of losing his wife (she died in a plane crash) and the struggle of raising his twin boys.

And then there's Eli Cash (Owen Wilson), faux cowboy extraordinaire, celebrity literary novelist (sort of a mix of Cormac McCarthy and Richard Brautigan) and a troubled childhood friend of the family. As a young man, Eli lived with his grandmother across the street – the proverbial boy from the 'wrong side of the tracks' who was forever peering into the looking glass of the Tenenbaum home. And while the clan's fortunes have dipped, Eli's have been soaring... until now. Eli's latest novel is a critical failure and his drug addiction is also raging out of control.

The three Tenenbaum children – who, despite their true ages, seem perpetually stuck in adolescence at the moment of their greatest triumphs – must begrudgingly come together (they all move back into the family brownstone) when their long-estranged father Royal returns to the fold after announcing that he is dying of stomach cancer. But when the truth is revealed via Etheline's new suitor, Henry Sherman (Danny Glover), that Royal isn't really dying of cancer – he only sought reconciliation with his family after being booted from the hotel he'd been living in for non-payment – the family splinters even further into despair and disarray.

Only three films in and Anderson had fine-tuned his visual style to a decorous polish while never letting the characters or emotion of a scene get lost. But for some critics, the refinement of this blatantly theatrical artifice coupled with the film's formal claustrophobic aesthetic – typically locking a character within the middle of the frame as a visual ornament more than a person – was not mannered so much as stiff and deathly self-conscious. Kenneth Turan, writing for the *Los Angeles Times*, stated that the film's obsession with detail had sucked all the life out of the performances: 'It is hard to find any connection points with such an insular, forbidding style, hard to find the hand-holds that make the climb inside possible.'[33] But others, like Jonathan Rosenbaum, found it 'one of the funniest comedies around'[34] despite having reservations about the heightened element of a cute factor.

It's not the easiest or most approachable film of his to settle into at first, but Anderson's technical sophistication matched with his ongoing love of the eccentric ensemble cast – roles now supplied by many who were firmly part of the Anderson troupe – offers up plenty of satisfaction with repeat viewings. Which is strangely a requirement for all of his films, though never more than for *The Royal Tenenbaums*, which has the narrative layers of a novel and comes equipped with chapter breaks and, of course, the previously mentioned narration by Baldwin. A novel, albeit one that comes with a killer mix-tape containing songs by Anderson's ubiquitous Rolling Stones, Nico, Van Morrison, Eliot Smith, along with a chamber music score by Anderson regular Mark Mothersbaugh.

The film would also continue Anderson's penchant for casting a veteran in a patriarchal role. The bearish Gene Hackman exudes just the right amount of con-man charm and Horatio Algeresque gumption tempered with a benevolence that keeps us begrudgingly on the side of the old bastard, even when we know he isn't worth it. Insulated by wealth and privilege (a common theme through all of Anderson's work), we know that selfish, washed-up Royal does not deserve to be let back into the family so easily. His attempts to understand his adult children at this stage are facile and comical. At one point he takes Margot to an ice cream parlour as if she were a little girl, and when he asks Richie about the televised meltdown during the tennis match, Royal's confusion over the incident is still focused on the load of money that he lost more than the mental health of his son. And yet, we still care. Hackman's performance is even more remarkable knowing the ongoing problems he had with Anderson during the production since the veteran actor was not always used to being fed line readings or subordinate to the meticulous set design and exacting compositions.

As with all of Anderson's work, much of the credit must be shared with cinematographer Robert Yeoman and production designer David Wasco, who both colour and give texture to this alien, fairytale New York of the mind. Although it was filmed on location in the city, New York takes on a shape and kineticism that is pure fiction, a sort of heightened reality – more the way we remember a place being than how it really is. From the autumnal leaves and Gypsy Cabs to the high-rise tennis courts, sidewalk crap games and punk rockers on the subway to a falcon's perch atop the Tenenbaum home – these are the images that many non-New Yorkers have of the city, drawn from television shows, books, movies, and photographs. This is a snapshot New York City, transposed through the lens of secondary sources though still natural enough for the viewer to latch on to, much like a dream which oscillates between the vibrantly 'real' and completely artificial.

Released in December 2001, the film garnered plenty of critical accolades and was a success at the box office, earning close to $72,000,000 worldwide. Topping many a critic's Year's Best, Anderson and Wilson were both nominated for a 2002 Best Writing/Screenplay Oscar, and Gene Hackman won the 2002 Golden Globe for Best Actor in a Musical or Comedy.

But while the afterglow was strong and heady for Anderson and company, stormy waters were about to plunge the filmmaker into what many feel was his first real failure…

The Life Aquatic with Steve Zissou (2004)

Directed by: Wes Anderson
Written by: Wes Anderson, Noah Baumbach
Produced by: Wes Anderson, Barry Mendel, Scott Rudin
Edited by: David Moritz
Cinematography by: Robert Yeoman
Cast: Bill Murray, Owen Wilson, Cate Blanchett, Anjelica Huston, Willem Dafoe, Jeff Goldblum, Michael Gambon, Bud Cort

'I wonder if it remembers me.' – Steve Zissou (Bill Murray) finally encounters the magnificent, mythical jaguar shark that ate his friend, Esteban (Seymour Cassel).

After the success of *The Royal Tenenbaums*, Wes Anderson embarked on the most ambitious, expensive and troubled production he had yet directed. It would also be the first time that Anderson and Owen Wilson would not collaborate on the script (due to Wilson's hectic acting career starring in various Hollywood blockbusters), though Wilson would have a prominent acting role in the film playing team leader Steve Zissou's long lost 'illegitimate' son, Edward 'Ned' Plimpton. The film would also have a bigger budget (estimated at $50,000,000) than the previous films, giving Anderson and crew the opportunity to relocate the production to the famed Cinecittà film studios in Rome. Superbly utilising the spaciousness of the soundstages, the film contains many spectacular sets such as a halved version of Zissou's ship the *Belafonte*, which allows us to peer inside to see all of the cabins and research areas, much like Godard's theatrical sausage factory set in *Tout va bien*. The surrounding Mediterranean region gave the film an openness and scope that was sometimes absent in Anderson's previous films.

With the larger budget, though, many critics (as well as fans) sensed that Anderson's vision had finally run aground, burdened by the film's bloat, meandering narrative and relentless fetishism with regard to detail. Worst of all, many felt it simply wasn't funny. No film of Anderson's has split his supporters so thoroughly with regard to its merit. David Edelstein – not exactly the biggest fan of Anderson in the first place – wrote in *Slate* that '…even a lot of Wes-worshippers concede that this one is a mess – a misshapen, mawkish tragicomedy bordering on self-parody'.[35] Richard Schickel, on the other hand, wrote that the film was the best American comedy of 2004 and that beneath its evasive humour and synthetic surface, the 'film is not as irrelevant as it dreamily pretends to be'.[36]

Although it's no more self-contained or stylised than any of his other films, there is a real looseness to *Life Aquatic* that reminds one of

Bottle Rocket. The plot, as simple and direct as they come, concerns Zissou's mad Ahab-like quest to hunt down and destroy the legendary jaguar shark that killed his best friend and loyal comrade. Zissou, who is explicitly and affectionately modelled after famed French explorer and filmmaker Jacques-Yves Cousteau, is no longer at the height of his career. In fact, Team Zissou is in the dumps. The ship and equipment are obsolete, though still working more or less (the electricity keeps shorting), funding for projects is drying up, the documentaries (horribly staged and peculiarly dated) are no longer generating mainstream viability, Zissou's marriage is falling apart, and his crew spends most of their time on the ship hanging out and watching old videos of their past endeavours, living vicariously through secondary sources. Zissou is, in effect, a man overboard.

But with the unexpected arrival of a Kentucky airline pilot named Ned, claiming to be the illegitimate son of Zissou, the project to hunt down the shark takes a turn for the better when Ned offers to finance part of the deal. Now with Ned, a 'bond company stooge' (Bud Cort) and a British magazine reporter (Cate Blanchett) penning a flaws-and-all profile of the explorer all on board, Team Zissou is back in action. How long the whole endeavour can stay afloat, though, is a whole other question.

The Life Aquatic is at times a beautiful, translucent jellyfish of a film. With its surreal underwater landscapes and digital sea creatures, Mark Mothersbaugh's Casio-tinged original score, Seu Jorge's acoustic Bowie covers sung in Portuguese (Jorge is also a member of the crew), creaky downgraded equipment, deliberate anti-action set pieces (including an attack by South Seas pirates and Team Zissou's rescuing of their chief rival Captain Hennessy, played by Jeff Goldblum) that resemble one of Zissou's own movie posters, and an ensemble cast that appropriately harks back to the wonderfully eccentric faces and personalities that once filled Fellini's frames, Anderson's ode to middle-age despair and redemption feels kooky and meaningful and unlike anything else you have seen. It's the true misfit among his work, the bruised and misunderstood colossus that is far from the misguided failure many believe it to be. In light of *The Darjeeling Limited*, the film looks more like a true transitional work, a film willingly changing the focus from youthful failure to middle-aged delusions and the imperative of shedding those delusions before mortality catches up with you – the presence of death being the film's great unnamed character.

Like most of Anderson's work, especially his last three films, death is significant and enters these comedic stories swiftly, without mercy, and is never cheaply deployed despite the cavalier desire to make the audience feel. Whether it's Buckley the dog in *The Royal Tenenbaums* (granted, played for laughs) setting up the off-camera demise of Royal (matter-of-factly reported by narrator Alec Baldwin), Ned's death in *Life Aquatic* or the spectre of their father's tragic fatal accident that haunts the three brothers in *The Darjeeling Limited* and the subsequent drowning of the Indian boy, death frequently becomes the catalyst for Anderson's characters to realise (if only for a moment) their own insignificance within a life worth living. Although death in and of itself does not always deliver profundity. Zissou uses the death of his comrade Esteban as a way to continue living as an 11-and-a-half-year old (his favourite year, he states at one point) and to not face reality. Only with Ned's death does Zissou react with confusion, pain and an unbearable rawness. Although hurt by the loss of Esteban, Zissou was able to incorporate the tragedy into the Zissou legend; yet another chapter within the packaged myth. But with Ned, Zissou is turned inside out, forced to be humbled before the unknowable dark mystery beyond. Submerged hundreds of feet below the waves within the explorer capsule, surrounded by friends and enemies alike, Zissou journeys through innerspace and toward the Big Inevitable much like Keir Dullea travelled toward his own consciousness shift in Kubrick's *2001: A Space Odyssey* (1968).

It's an adventurous moment indeed, and further evidence that beneath the formalism, the plastic, the finely wrought moments of irony and emotional reticence beats the heart of a guerrilla sentimentalist.

The Darjeeling Limited (2007)

Directed by: Wes Anderson
Written by: Wes Anderson, Roman Coppola, Jason Schwartzman
Produced by: Wes Anderson, Roman Coppola, Lydia Dean Pilcher, Scott Rudin
Edited by: Andrew Weisblum
Cinematography by: Robert Yeoman
Cast: Owen Wilson, Adrien Brody, Jason Schwartzman, Anjelica Huston, Waris Ahuwalia, Amara Karan, Irfan Khan

'Is that symbolic? We. Haven't. Located. Us. Yet!' – Francis Whitman (Owen Wilson) has his mind blown when he realises that the train he and his brothers have been passengers on is lost.

Anderson has never been averse to addressing mortality head-on in his films, specifically the death of a spouse (*Rushmore*), parent (*The Royal Tenenbaums*) or child (*The Life Aquatic with Steve Zissou*). Although all of his films are ostensibly comedies, there has always been an element of the impermanence of things, of people, that has delicately coaxed an emotional resonance forth from the wackiness. Not particularly original or groundbreaking, but when one considers the frequently bathetic treatment of death in much of American mainstream cinema, Anderson's unsentimental and realistic treatment of grief is a commendable aspect and intrusion upon his lucid, intensely fabricated theatricality. As much as Anderson has become a master of the elaborate, multi-layered *mise-en-scène*, he also astutely understands the moment to drop back, allowing his characters to feel the brunt of their sorrow without excessive ornamentation. *The Darjeeling Limited* is as waggish as any of Anderson's previous work. But at its core is the black hole of loss, the invisible thread that binds us as profoundly (if not more so) than birth.

By this point, it's impossible to remain neutral about the films of Wes Anderson. You either find his work 'precocious', 'quirky', 'self-conscious' and 'unfunny' or delight in its finely crafted, intentional artificiality, heightened realism, exaggerated characters and open-hearted emotion. *The Darjeeling Limited* is not a major departure from Anderson's previous work, but it is the most focused, relaxed and stripped-down production since *Bottle Rocket*, while still delivering the same visual hallmarks and familiar themes that he has obsessed over throughout his career. It's also his most mature film to date – a discerning trip into matters of frayed fraternal obligation and the possibility of friendship beyond the bloodline.

Written by Anderson, Roman Coppola and Jason Schwartzman, the film focuses on three brothers, all typically Andersonian adult-children of indeterminate wealth and privilege (like characters out of a 1930s screwball comedy), who have not been in contact with one another since the death of their father a year earlier, but have now reunited to take a train trip through India in order to mend their relationship and find enlightenment. Francis, the de facto leader of the group, still healing from an attempted suicide attempt, tries to micromanage their every move with a daily itinerary made up by his assistant Brendan (Wallace Wolodarsky), who travels with the group but in a different compartment of the train. The daily plans, which are always laminated and slipped underneath the cabin door, instruct the brothers as to what holy temples to visit and when to eat, rigidly defining the brothers' every movement. Peter (Adrien Brody), the married one of the group and a reluctant expectant father, is also the brother closest to making a significant belated leap into full adulthood because of his impending role as a parent. And then there is Jack the lothario (Schwartzman), a heartsick literary writer who has spent the last few months living in exile in a swanky Parisian hotel after suffering a painful break-up with his girlfriend (Natalie Portman), which is the subject of the short film *Hotel Chevalier* that serves as a significant and telling prologue to *The Darjeeling Limited*.

But the brothers' 'spiritual journey' is fraught with comical miscalculations, arguments and painful recriminations that eventually find the three men kicked off the train and alone in the wilds of India. Stripped of their pretensions of enlightenment, comfort and wealth, they reach rock bottom when a tragic incident sweeps them out of their own neurosis, forcing them to confront their own fragile predicament. The journey does not end there, though. Unbeknownst to Jack or Peter, Francis intends to lead them to their estranged mother (Anjelica Huston), who is now a nun living in an abbey in the shadow of the Himalayas (a nod to Michael Powell's 1947 film *Black Narcissus*), despite her refusal to see them because of a man-eating tiger in the area.

Much of the film, especially in the second half, plays like a feminised, seriocomic take on *Apocalypse Now*, with the brothers journeying toward their confrontation with mom – complete with unforeseen detours both ludicrous and dire – who they feel has somehow betrayed them by failing to attend their father's funeral and willingly isolating herself from the world, like some selfish though charitable Colonel Kurtz. But the brothers' plans are thwarted yet again when she dismisses their accusations as selfish and wrong, opening the doorway to a hopeful *tabula rasa*. The Whitman brothers are really searching for meaning, a glimmer of understanding within the fog of the past that they have been unable to steer through with clear eyes. Only when their mission is taken out of their hands, 'to be continued' as their mother intones before bedtime prior to disappearing from their lives again (she goes off to kill the tiger), are the brothers free at last to decide their own failure or success. There are no pithy resolutions at the end of the journey, no profound moment of clarity. There is just the realisation that one is alive in the moment and that a new journey awaits where one unexpectedly ends. After the brothers are abandoned at the abbey, they climb a mountain and improvise a ritual to celebrate their new bond (something they attempted to do earlier in the film to comical results) before literally jumping aboard a train bound for new adventures.

The light and space of India generate a new palette for Anderson to draw from, adding a dusty grit and dimension to his usual meticulous design schemes. It's a welcome looseness, as is the incorporation of music cues pulled from numerous films of Satyajit Ray (whose films made Anderson want to film in India in the first place) and Merchant-

Ivory, which add an appropriate organic texture that Anderson's regular music composer Mark Mothersbaugh would not have been able to reproduce. And while Anderson's beloved the Rolling Stones and the Kinks are represented – the use of the Stones' 'Playing with Fire' during the silent reconciliation sequence between the brothers and their mother is a sublimely virtuosic moment – the usual British Invasion stylings are kept to a minimum.

After its premiere at the Venice and New York film festivals, the film opened to initially strong US box office and received some of the best reviews for one of Anderson's pictures, many finding it a welcome return to form after the perceived failure of *The Life Aquatic*. But with the praise came the requisite scorn, including accusations of racism, namely from *Slate* writer Jonah Weiner who blasted the film as Anderson's 'most obnoxious movie yet'.[37] Admittedly race has sometimes been a tricky issue in Anderson's films, even though he consistently uses large, multi-ethnic ensembles. There is an air of cultural exoticism to the portrayal of minorities that can often come across as patronising because Anderson consistently simplifies them as inherently good people. However, what makes the accusations hollow is the fact that Anderson views all of his characters through the same elastic, comedic lens, not turning them into caricatures so much as exaggerating the inherent goodness he sees within *all* of his misfits, much like Renoir, Truffaut and Charles M. Schulz did in their own ways. And if that is an artistic crime, then Anderson is guilty as charged.

SPIKE JONZE

'Yes, there is an American New Wave and it's exactly like the rest of
America – casual, brilliant, spoiled, ironic, and devoutly youthful.'
– David Thomson on Spike Jonze[38]

Spike Jonze is the Bugs Bunny of cinema. A chameleon trickster capable of delivering inspired, surreal feints while setting the stage for a
strange lyricism and poignancy that eases toward an imaginative transcendence of the quotidian reminiscent of Buñuel, though without the
social or political contexts. Pretty good for a huckster who was born
as Adam Spiegel in 1969 and is a distant relative to the Spiegel family
(they of the mail-order fortune), though not apparently an heir despite
what many an early biography has stated.

A child of divorced parents, the teenaged Jonze eventually fell in
with a group of skateboarders and BMX obsessives who tempted fate
and physics at every turn. His passion for skateboarding and freestyle
riding would eventually land him a job writing and taking photographs
for the magazine *Freestylin'* while still in high school, and later he
would find work as a photographer with *Transworld Skateboarding*
magazine, in the late 1980s. And in 1991, Jonze would direct his first
real film, the underground skateboarding classic, *Video Days*, which
chronicled the insane freestylin' antics of the Blind Skateboard team.
The film would subsequently land him work directing music videos
such as the promo for Sonic Youth's *100%* (1992), co-directed with
Tamra Davis, showing in cinéma vérité style urban skateboarders riding on balustrades, down concrete stairs and performing other death-

defying stunts, as well as lead to his active participation in the wildly successful *Jackass* television show for MTV and later movies. In the early 1990s, Jonze also became co-editor of *Dirt, Sassy* magazine's publication for teenage boys.

But his entry into film came via music promos. Throughout the 1990s, Jonze infused the art of the music video with a successive array of distinctive absurdist concepts with a charming surrealist bent that set them apart even within a format that was founded on abstract surrealist imagery and operatic storylines. In many respects, this second wave of music video directors that flourished in the 1990s – David Fincher, Jonathan Glazer, Mark Romanek, Chris Cunningham, Peter Care, Michel Gondry, Spike Jonze, et al – elevated the form to a whole new level of stylistic brilliance whether they were utilising the latest technology for big-budget concepts or stripping it down for a more street-level, lo-fi uniqueness. Jonze's video work, ranging from promos for the alternative rock bands the Breeders ('Cannonball', 'Divine Hammer'), Teenage Fanclub ('Hang On'), Pavement ('Shady Lane'), Dinosaur Jr. ('Feel the Pain'), REM ('Crush with Eyeliner'), Tenacious D (the epic 'Wonderboy'), Wax ('California', containing one of his most resonant images, that of a man on fire serenely running down a city street) and Weezer ('Buddy Holly', 'Undone-The Sweater Song', the former a hilarious pastiche of the 1970s television show *Happy Days*) to his frequent collaborations with the Beastie Boys ('Sabotage', a hilarious take on cheesy television cop shows), Björk ('It's Oh So Quiet', a wonderful homage to Demy's *Les Parapluies de Cherbourg*) to perhaps his greatest moment of deliberate comedic provocation for Fatboy Slim's 'Praise You', wherein the director (as choreographer Richard Koufey) leads the fictional Torrance Community Dance Group on a guerrilla campaign of improvisatory dance on the streets of Hollywood. The resulting low-budget video (co-directed with Roman Coppola), which astonishingly went on to win three awards at the 1999 MTV Music Video Awards (Best Video, Best Direction and Best Choreography), felt like a stealthy mix of Andy Kaufman-esque anti-comedy and Artaud's Theatre of Cruelty, infused with an abundant amiableness that has continued throughout his feature film work. Has there been a finer moment in the history of the MTV Awards? Certainly not.

During this time, Jonze also worked on a number of commercials for Lee Jeans, Coca-Cola and Nike. His ad for Levi's jeans, in which a horribly injured accident victim is whisked into a hospital emergency room then bursts into a rendition of Soft Cell's cover of 'Tainted Love' with the hospital staff falling in suit, is another highlight of Jonze's short work.

Jonze finally made the leap to feature filmmaking in 1997 when he was offered the script of *Being John Malkovich*, written by a then relatively unknown screenwriter named Charlie Kaufman. The script, which was being shopped around Hollywood by REM singer Michael Stipe's production company, Single Cell Pictures, eventually found its way to Jonze not long after what was intended to be his first feature, *Harold and the Purple Crayon*, based on the classic children's book by Crockett Johnson, fell apart when TriStar Pictures was no longer interested.[39]

The collaboration between Jonze and Kaufman is a watershed moment in American film. And while other subversively minded films were being released into the mainstream that same year – Sam Mendes' *American Beauty*, Kimberly Peirce's *Boys Don't Cry*, Kevin Smith's *Dogma*, Alexander Payne's *Election*, David Fincher's *Fight Club*, P.T. Anderson's *Magnolia*, David O. Russell's *Three Kings* (co-starring Jonze as backwoods hick, Private Conrad Vig) and Sofia Coppola's *The Virgin Suicides* – the twisted, lyrical beauty of Jonze and Kaufman's collaboration still elevated it to another level. If *Malkovich* was not necessarily the finest film of the lot, it was certainly the most audacious and original.

The press-shy Jonze subsequently found himself in the limelight after the release of the film, and it was also during this time that he married Hollywood royalty, fellow filmmaker Sofia Coppola, who he had met while directing the Sonic Youth video. But in less than four years the couple would divorce.

After turning down the chance to direct *Human Nature* with Kaufman (the director's chair going to Michel Gondry instead), Jonze and Kaufman re-teamed for *Adaptation* (2002), a sometimes extraordinary meta-fictional examination of a screenwriter named Charlie Kaufman (Nicolas Cage) who is hired to adapt the bestselling non-fiction book *The Orchid Thief*, by Susan Orlean (Meryl Streep), into a movie in the wake of the wild success of the film *Being John Malkovich*. Problem is, Kaufman – who lives with his aspiring screenwriter twin, Donald (Nicolas Cage) – can't figure out how to adapt the unwieldy book into a commercial film. Even more delirious and genre imploding than *Malkovich*, the film is an assured follow-up, even though it careens into a swamp of cynicism and narrative confusion in its last act. The film, nevertheless, showed a new maturity for Jonze and solidified him as a careful and strangely restrained filmmaker, intuitively allowing the naturalistic elements of the script to rise to the surface so as not to force the more outré components. For a director with such a taste for the brazenly fantastical, he also has the intelligence and steadiness of a filmmaker who understands the worthy power of subtlety as well.

Jonze's latest project is a live-action adaptation of Maurice Sendak's classic children's picture book, *Where the Wild Things Are*, scripted by author and founder of the *McSweeny's* literary journal, Dave Eggers. The film, due to be released in October 2008 by Warner Bros., stars Catherine Keener, Forrest Whitaker, James Gandolfini, Paul Dano, Michelle Williams, Catherine O'Hara, Tom Noonan and Max Records as Max, the mischievous though courageous boy who dons a wolf suit and journeys to the land of the Wild Things after being sent to bed without any dinner by his parents. The book is a bounty of feral imagination and deceptively simple storytelling, offering up plenty of nuances that have endeared it to children the world over, even while their parents, appropriately enough, fail to get it. The first feature that Jonze and Kaufman have not collaborated on, it will be interesting to see if this cinematic Max Records, with his special brand of sophisticated child-like wonder combined with a fearless approach to conveying rather bizarre concepts to a wide audience, can still deliver.

Although the eyes of the world focused more on Spike Jonze after the release of *Being John Malkovich* – no doubt stemming from the still unvanquished idea for many filmgoers that the director is absolute ruler, miraculously creating the entire film in true Herculean fashion – it slowly became apparent that the remarkable Jonze was not the chief visionary of the work but an intelligent conduit for Kaufman's ideas, words, and vision. Kaufman *not* Jonze is arguably the true *auteur* of their films together. And this has become even more clear as Kaufman has gone on to work with Michel Gondry, a director who also has a prodigious ability to convey true wonderment and fantasy upon the screen.

Being John Malkovich (1999)

Directed by: Spike Jonze
Written by: Charlie Kaufman
Produced by: Steve Golin, Vincent Landay, Sandy Stern, Michael Stipe
Edited by: Eric Zumbrunnen
Cinematography by: Lance Acord
Cast: John Cusack, Cameron Diaz, Catherine Keener, John Malkovich, Orson Bean, Mary Kay Place

'I have been to the dark side and back. I have seen a world that no man should see.' – John Malkovich (John Malkovich), disturbed after journeying through the portal into his own head.

It was the spark that started it all. Of course, the film's lineage can be traced back to the fantasy/surrealist films of Luis Buñuel and Terry Gilliam, the stories of Jorge Luis Borges as well as Philip K. Dick, among others. Perhaps the shock of the new has worn off over the last decade. Though that has less to do with the film itself than with how the culture at large has adapted and assimilated the weird, surreal and strange textures into its fictions, be they television advertisements, music videos – both being the original playgrounds for director Spike Jonze – or other films that stretch into the fantastic without being necessarily traditional fantasy genre fare. In the post-Charlie Kaufman years, mainstream pop culture seems even more inundated with the metafictional and a sort of trickle-down post-modernism than ever before, to the point where the casual viewer hardly raises an eyebrow. It's to the credit of Jonze and Kaufman's originality that, despite the permutation of the surreal in everyday life, *Being John Malkovich* still feels fresh, bizarre, and funny.

All great fantasy stories, be they films or print, must adhere to their own logic and tether to an approximation of physics and the natural order of things if the images are to successfully seduce us into their own cinematic reality, sway us into their spell of illogic. Jonze and Kaufman's film is no different. By thoroughly grounding the characters within a recognisable, naturalistic world – the NYC of daily commutes, office drudgery, cramped apartment life, the profusion of media and celebrity in all of our lives – the film's off-the-cuff verisimilitude (shot by Lance Acord) becomes the perfect foundation in which to unleash the more absurd plot elements and comedic genius of the premise that a portal hidden in the wall behind a file cabinet inside a non descript Manhattan office is actually a passage into actor John Malkovich's head.

Pressured by his wife Lotte (Cameron Diaz), street puppeteer Craig Schwartz (John Cusack) – who with his marionettes performs vignettes chronicling the correspondence between the tragic medieval lovers Heloise and Abelard – begrudgingly lays down his toys in order to seek out more substantial and lucrative work. Craig does find work as a file clerk working for LesterCorp, a strange file company located on the seventh and a half floor of the Mertin-Flemmer building in downtown Manhattan, run by the equally strange Mr. Lester (Orson Bean). One day, while routinely filing some papers away, Craig discovers by accident a passageway in the wall hidden behind one of the cabinets. And like a modern-day Alice in Wonderland... he crawls through, discovering that the tunnel leads miraculously into the head of Malkovich, giving him the unbelievable opportunity to experience the world through the actor's eyes, before spitting him out on the side of the New Jersey Turnpike. The experience, transcendent to say the least, changes Craig's life and he quickly gets Lotte to plunge down it as well as a co-worker, Maxine (Catherine Keener), who Craig lusts after. The ramifications of being John Malkovich are enormous for the trio and for Malkovich himself when he discovers, much to his metaphysical anguish, what is going on.

The magnitude of being the notoriously difficult and talented character actor was not lost on audiences either. Not only did the film launch Kaufman and Jonze into the mainstream, it also blurred the respective genres (science fiction, fantasy, comedy, the avant-garde) into something unique yet accessible. It was a film unafraid to visualise the absurd or risk being foolish, offering up complex ideas about identity (sexual or otherwise), celebrity (Malkovich, behind closed doors, is completely average and as lonely as everyone else) and the eternal life of chimps. Ridiculous, moving, cartoonish, serious and hilarious, the film's true masterstroke scene – the moment that propels it into the realm of the brilliant – is when Malkovich sneaks into the Mertin-Flemmer building and joins the long line of consumers who are paying Craig and Maxine to spend fifteen minutes being Malkovich. Completely outraged, Malkovich demands to crawl through the portal wherein he discovers that everyone in the world truly is a reflection of himself. Like the best moments with Kaufman, the scene works as a perfectly timed comedic gag and a queasy metaphysical conundrum. And the longer one ponders such questions, the deeper one falls into the indescribable joke of it all.

Adaptation (2002)

Directed by: Spike Jonze
Written by: Charlie Kaufman
Produced by: Jonathan Demme, Vincent Landay, Edward Saxon
Edited by: Eric Zumbrunnen
Cinematography by: Lance Acord
Cast: Nicolas Cage, Meryl Streep, Chris Cooper, Tilda Swinton, Ron Livingston, Brian Cox, Maggie Gyllenhaal

'I don't want to cram in sex or guns or car chases or characters learning profound life lessons or growing or coming to like each other or overcome obstacles to succeed in the end. The book isn't like that, and life isn't like that, it just isn't.' – Charlie Kaufman (Nicolas Cage) on how *not* to end the script he is struggling to adapt from the book *The Orchid Thief*, by Susan Orlean (Meryl Streep).

'...they're so mutable. Adaptation is a profound process. Means you figure out how to thrive in the world.' – The orchid thief, John Larouch (Chris Cooper), speaks with Orlean.

Narrative egomania. *Adaptation*, a blissfully absurdist, self-reflexive, comedy about screenwriter Charlie Kaufman's traumatic attempt to adapt Susan Orlean's bestselling book, *The Orchid Thief*, for the screen in the wake of *Being John Malkovich*'s success, is about as self-absorbed, narcissistic and pointed as films get about the creative inner struggles that a writer faces every time they sit down and stare at the whiteness of the page. There have been numerous films that have used the inner turmoil of the wordsmith for cinematic fodder – *Sunset Boulevard* (1950), *The Day of the Locust* (1975), *The Singing Detective* (1986), *Mishima* (1985), *Barton Fink* (1991), *Naked Lunch* (1991), *Deconstructing Harry* (1997), *Wonder Boys* (2000), *Swimming Pool* (2003), and *Sideways* (2004) are just a few that come to mind. A disparate group of films to say the least, but each one of them conveys in some manner the inner weirdness, terror, excitement, and boredom of a writer's life. But none of them plunges so deeply or blatantly into the actual mental anguish of the cerebral writing process itself, the actual painstaking, solitary drudgery of making words sing upon a page, than Kaufman and Jonze's film.

America loves its larger-than-life, cinematic heroes, be they real or imagined. John Wayne, Ronald Reagan, Clint Eastwood, Rocky, Rambo, Luke Skywalker, Indiana Jones, Schwarzenegger, Spider-Man, and Superman have all nestled comfortably within the collective American psyche, mirroring our fascination with characters or actors who supposedly represent the ideal upstanding, hardworking citizen hero. But American cinema also shares a preoccupation and fascination with the lovable loser, the schulb, the socially maladjusted dork you feel sorry for but still go out of your way to miss, if you notice him at all. Guys like Charlie and Donald Kaufman in *Adaptation*.

Hollywood has always had its fair share of lovable comedic losers to choose from: whether Chaplin and Keaton during the heyday of the silents, Jerry Lewis in the 1950s or Jim Carrey and Ben Stiller today, audiences generally love the intrepid loser. Woody Allen in the 1970s became a patron saint of loserdom, a sexy auteur of silliness and neurosis for many. But while mainstream audiences have generally been receptive to the comic social slouch (just as long as he's not too weird), the independent film has been a much more receptive habitat for the outright creepy guy. In recent years, films such as *Happiness* (1998), *Chuck & Buck, Tao of Steve* (2000), *Ghost World* and *American Splendor* (2003) – the latter film based on the very real Harvey Pekar, the Cleveland-based alternative comic book writer – have all featured variants of the 'loser' model, though none perhaps as revealing and brutally honest as Kaufman's fictional interpretation of himself.

Kaufman's work is filled with intelligent people who regularly grapple with feeling physically inadequate, shy, depressed, unmotivated and confused, among many other things. Some of them are employed in dreary jobs – clerical, retail, office work, game-show host – and many of them could be construed as losers, freaks and weirdos. But the biggest loser in the Kaufman canon may be screenwriter Charlie Kaufman himself and his fictional brother, Donald (also played by Nicolas Cage), who in the film is living with Charlie and attempting to write his own screenplay entitled *The 3*, a by-the-numbers psychological serial-killer opus in which a police investigator, a serial killer and a female hostage are all the same person.[40] Both brothers are fat, balding, single, and in the case of Charlie, a chronic masturbator. Charlie, who is agonising over the adaptation of Orlean's book, valiantly tries to write something original, intelligent, and meaningful, but suffers writer's block in his attempt. Donald – who is earnest and generally uncomplicated, basically what Charlie isn't – becomes an extension of Charlie's worst fears, his worst desire to 'sell out' to Hollywood and the barrier that keeps him from making a vital artistic statement. While Charlie struggles with the script and with women, Donald breezes through his own mechanical screenplay (using screenwriting guru Robert McKee's books and lessons as a template) and winds up dating a woman named Caroline (Maggie Gyllenhaal), a make-up artist on the set of *Being John Malkovich*. But Donald and McKee (Brian Cox) eventually become inadvertent saviours for Charlie. And by the end, while the film's narrative and viewer expectations take a delirious detour into the Florida swamps where the horticulturist Larouch, Orlean and the fate of Charlie's script await, the value and meaning of cultivating an obsession becomes a little clearer amidst the plunge into melodrama.

As with their previous collaboration, *Being John Malkovich*, Jonze and Kaufman excel at the art of the con (there is no Donald Kaufman), the prank (Charlie Kaufman is not the Charlie Kaufman from the film), and the brilliant diversion (the film's final act in which Kaufman manages to commit all of the artistic sins he swore *not* to commit). But *Adaptation* is no mere gimmick, some cinematic Houdini out to rob us of our patience. Underneath the layers of accumulated neurosis, beneath the serpentine plot twists and scathing satire, is a film of wondrous poetry, vision and subtlety, a film filled with expertly timed dialogue, career-best performances (Cage, Streep and Cooper are all exemplary), and a complexity and lightness of touch that are rare in Hollywood. There's patience in Jonze's frames, a trust that the actors inhabiting the scene are likewise adapting to the material in ways that are completely invigorating, fresh and unique, as if they too are searching for a way out of the familiar, a way to escape the confines of the American comedy genre without sacrificing laughs.

The film, financed and released by Columbia Pictures, was another hit for Jonze and Kaufman, solidifying their status as the most original new voices in American cinema. Both were either nominated for or won numerous awards that year, including the BAFTA for Best Adapted Screenplay, and Spike Jonze was awarded the prestigious

Silver Bear at the 2003 Berlin International Film Festival. Chris Cooper also won the Academy Award for Best Supporting Actor, while Nicolas Cage was nominated for his portrayal of the two brothers.

Despite the film's mostly glowing reviews and reception, there were voices of dissension, like the vitriolic attack by Robert Wilonsky in the *Dallas Observer* who felt the film was 'the most overrated movie of the year (of all time?)'[41] and 'lazy and solipsistic'. Jonathan Rosenbaum *did* enjoy the film, though the *Chicago Reader* critic also found fault with the film's final third as a road to 'nowhere'.

SOFIA COPPOLA

'Coming from my family and having connections definitely helps open doors. But then once you're there, you have to come through.'
– Sofia Coppola[42]

'Reactionary, poetic, sparkling, ebullient, effervescent, fragrant, cold, cool, coming of age, bestowing of presence, petulant and revolutionary' – The label, written by Francis Ford Coppola, on the sparkling wine named after his daughter.

She is the daughter of the great American filmmaker Francis Ford Coppola, and with only three films under her belt so far, Sofia Coppola has already begun to carve out her own modest legacy. For many, she represents the epitome of Hollywood chic – a jet-setting daughter of a genuine Hollywood maverick; niece to actress Talia Shire; cousin to actors Nicolas Cage and Jason Schwartzman (the latter being Shire's son); sometime actress in her father's films; fashion designer; heiress to the family wine fortune (she even has a sparkling wine named after her); award-winning director of films about… well, people much like herself, or at least what the public thinks she is like. And for others she represents the worst aspects of Hollywood nepotism – a jet-setting daughter of a genuine Hollywood maverick; sometime actress in her father's films; fashion designer; heiress; award-winning film director.

Even though Sofia Coppola has not appeared in one of her father's films since *The Godfather, Part III* (1990), her role as Michael Corleone's daughter Mary – originally written with Winona Ryder in mind – still lingers for many as the film's great misstep. Coppola had been in her father's films before, though always relegated to nothing more than a glimpse here or a walk-on there. The gangly young girl billed herself as 'Domino' because she thought the name sounded glamorous. But never had young Sofia been put in a position to really have to act, given a major role within such a highly visible and prestigious production as a *Godfather* film (she was, though, cast as the baptised baby at the end of the first film, and in the second film as an immigrant child on a ship bound for New York).

Reviews were harsh and brutal regarding Coppola's supposed miscasting (there's no doubt that she is out of her league, but her performance nevertheless is appropriately awkward and tenderly vulnerable), and the scathing critical comments – which felt at times like outright personal attacks aimed at Francis himself – were reminiscent of another famous Hollywood director's daughter and her first foray into film acting. In 1969, a 16-year-old Anjelica Huston had the misfortune of playing the lead in her father John Huston's misguided period romance, *A Walk with Love and Death* (1969). Critics pounced on the unskilled Anjelica and it would be 15 years before she tried tackling another substantial role (she wandered in and out of a few films in between), as Maerose Prizzi in her father's droll, mob black comedy, *Prizzi's Honour* (1985). Huston won the Academy Award for Best Supporting Actress for her work.

A lot has changed since Coppola was unjustly vilified for her father's casting blunder. For the most part, the younger Coppola retreated from the limelight to pursue other interests such as studying fine art at Cal Arts, starting a clothing line with close friend Stephanie Hayman, and then easing into the director's chair. Coppola's only previous legitimate behind-the-scenes work was co-writing with her father the excruciating Eloise pastiche and widely panned *Life Without Zoe* segment (also directed by her father) for the 1989 anthology film *New York Stories*, also featuring short films by Martin Scorsese and Woody Allen. A year later she also designed the 1970s-era costumes for the comedy *The Spirit of '76* (1990), co-written by her brother Roman Coppola.

Then came the well-regarded, black-and-white short film *Lick the Star* in 1998, about a group of teenage girls who conspire to weed out the boy population at their school with rat poison, after getting the idea from the V.C. Andrews novel *Flowers in the Attic* (a touchstone for many an adolescent American girl). But after a few of the girls learn about slavery in the US in the 1800s, they turn on their ringleader. Coppola co-wrote the film with Stephanie Hayman, foreshadowing a similar strain of teenage girl fetishisation – sans ennui – that she would explore more thoroughly in her next film. *Lick the Star* also marked the first time Coppola and cinematographer Lance Acord would collaborate, though his work here is far more straightforward than the cool, dreamy textures that gave *Lost in Translation* and *Marie Antoinette* much of their cosmetic allure.

Coppola then directed her first feature film, *The Virgin Suicides* (1999), based on the acclaimed novel by Jeffrey Eugenides. Laid-back, spacey, with just the right touch of teenage-nova daydream to float through the grim storyline about five preternaturally beautiful sisters who inexplicably kill themselves – forever haunting the young boys who knew them from afar – the film was a confident debut and well received critically.

Regardless of the good notices, accusations of nepotism reared their ugly head once again (Francis Ford Coppola was a producer on the film). Not that Coppola seemed to care. Instead, she set to work on what would ultimately solidify her as an accomplished filmmaker in her own right and a keen observer of the empty spaces (both physical and mental) that many of us drift in and out of, hoping to find a glimmer of a chance to connect with another person. The result, *Lost in Translation* (2003), would catapult actress Scarlett Johansson into the celebrity stratosphere, helped resurrect comedian Bill Murray for a whole new generation (Murray's role in Wes Anderson's *Rushmore* also contributed to this in a major way) and garnered the film, its stars, and its director numerous awards including a 2004 Best Original

Screenplay Oscar for Coppola. She was also only the third woman to ever be nominated for the Best Director award, after Italy's Lina Wertmüller for *Pasqualino Settebellezze/Seven Beauties* (1975) and New Zealand's Jane Campion for *The Piano* (1993).

Coppola's most recent film is a biopic of the infamous aforementioned eighteenth-century Queen of France. Re-teamed with her *Virgin Suicides* starlet, Kirsten Dunst, Coppola got the opportunity to film her long-held dream project. But despite the smeared dreaminess, committed attention to historical design detail and some effulgent moments of tenderness toward the routinely despised young queen, the film received a raucous beating at the 2006 Cannes Film Festival that only served as a warning for the critical backlash that followed.

In an industry where sexism still flourishes, where movie studios routinely retire actresses to the 'mom' role as they near 40 or demote them to television roles, where presidents of production for major studios proclaim that they '...are no longer doing movies with women in the lead'[43] and where the ubiquitous and patronising 'chick flick' romantic comedies that come somersaulting out of the studio gates are cynically deemed the kind of fare that all women are expected to consume regardless of any artistic worth, Sofia Coppola's modest cinematic confections are a bounty of satisfaction. And while her films are a far cry from the more ostentatious productions of her father, they do share a fixation on the role of family life to the individual. Though in the younger Coppola's work, family life is not viewed as a benevolent comfort. It is frequently seen as stifling and smothering, and only accentuates the isolation that her protagonists endure.

The Virgin Suicides (1999)

Directed by: Sofia Coppola
Written by: Sofia Coppola
Produced by: Francis Ford Coppola, Julie Costanzo, Dan Halsted, Chris Hanley
Edited by: Melissa Kent, James Lyons

Cinematography by: Edward Lachman
Cast: James Woods, Kathleen Turner, Kirsten Dunst, Josh Hartnett, Michael Paré, Scott Glenn, Danny DeVito, A.J. Cook, Hanna Hall, Leslie Hayman, Chelse Swain, Giovanni Ribisi

> 'What are you doing here, honey? You're not even old enough to know how bad life gets.'
> 'Obviously, Doctor, you've never been a 13-year-old girl.'
> – The youngest of the Lisbon sisters, Cecilia (Hanna Hall), speaks with secret wisdom.

The film grooves like an enigmatic, hazy, stoned recollection, which is what it essentially is. Based upon the novel by Jeffrey Eugenides, Coppola's translucent feature debut shimmers with a tenderness and brightness masking deep pain and regret, a confident and fluid evocation of upper-middle-class suburban life in the late 1970s, and the inexplicable suicides of the five Lisbon sisters and the spell that ensnares the unwary teenage boys fascinated by them. As wistfully narrated by actor Giovanni Ribisi (playing one of the boys now grown up), the film likewise casts an entrancing spell of its own, conjuring up sounds and visions of the past – cherry-flavoured lipstick, muscle cars, bubblegum pop (the film's soundtrack includes songs by Heart, the Hollies and Styx) and the feeling that we are peeking inside a teenage girl's diary, that we are coveting, fetishising moments that should be forbidden to us.

But Coppola's film, like Linklater's *Dazed and Confused*, is no empty-headed nostalgia trip. There's a certain fabulous darkness beating beneath its sugar-coated façade, a knowingness about the cryptic inner lives of these black swans that is rooted in mournful truth. No film, except for David Lynch's *Twin Peaks* series and Peter Jackson's *Heavenly Creatures* (1994), seems so unafraid to plunge the viewer into the dark emotional waters of female adolescence, to relinquish us into the bottomless well at the heart of the film. Although the presence of death permeates the film from the opening – 13-year-old Cecilia attempts suicide and a diseased tree in the front yard has been marked to be sawn down by the city – Coppola punctuates the film with moments of black humour and a willowy style that is intoxicating and drippy at the same time. Coating the film with the talismans of girly kitsch – unicorns, rainbows, shooting stars – Coppola offsets the creeping inevitability until she can't hold back any longer, and then seduces us into an empty void that resonates like a chilling urban legend. Like the teenage boys who find themselves smitten and bewildered by the girls' mystery, and who as men try to coax some sort of meaning from the tragedy like a form of sympathetic magic, we too are uncomprehending, lost and intoxicated in our attempts to decode their femininity.

The film unfolds like a fairytale rooted in myth, and much of its power is derived from those teenage artifacts it so ruthlessly exploits. But the performances are what hold the story together, keeping it from sinking into the miasma of meaningless nostalgia. Both James Woods and Kathleen Turner generate a painful sympathy in their roles as the strict and oppressive parents, who in their attempts to control and harness their daughters' weird currents, suffocate and ultimately trigger the inevitable. As the girls' clueless high school math-teaching father, able to contemplate the mystery of the universe better than fathom his daughters, Woods gives a strong and sympathetic portrait of a man who should have probably never become a father. As Lux – the mysterious, self-knowing guardian of the sisters – Kirsten Dunst captures a sort of mystic mundanity in her eyes and speech, especially when she becomes involved with the school stud, Trip Fontaine (Josh Hartnett), the prototypical stoner dude able to score the best girls and the best weed in school. Trip, who never really understood what he had with Lux, is even more incapable of understanding 25 years later when, as a fragile, burnt-out adult (played by Michael Paré), he pathetically looks back at his time with Lux as the best moment of his life. It's an accurate enough assessment, since the years of hard living have indeed taken their toll on Trip, but his obliviousness rings hollow when taking into account the fallout that awaits Lux and her sisters after the night on the football field with Trip, which in turn becomes the catalyst for the tragedy to come.

Except for the unnecessary coda which is taken from the book and feels symbolically heavy-handed and abrasive – a sequence after the suicides showing many of the affluent townsfolk at a party, ambivalent about the tragedy – the film remains a sometimes masterful blend of humour and elegiac moodiness. Although *The Virgin Suicides* was not a hit, critics generally liked the film and seemed ready to reassess Sofia Coppola after the unmitigated and out-of-proportion trouncing she received for her acting work in *The Godfather, Part III*. Good thing, since with her next picture the young director would make a lot more people take notice with an even more assured and worthy contribution to international film.

Lost in Translation (2003)

Directed by: Sofia Coppola
Written by: Sofia Coppola
Produced by: Ross Katz, Sofia Coppola
Edited by: Sarah Flack
Cinematography by: Lance Acord
Cast: Bill Murray, Scarlett Johansson, Giovanni Ribisi, Anna Faris

'You're probably just having a mid-life crisis. Did you buy a Porsche yet?' – Charlotte (Scarlett Johansson) fails to reassure her new friend Bob Harris (Bill Murray).

Sofia Coppola's sophomore film easily sidestepped any worries whether or not she could step out of her legendary father's shadow (he produced her first film and was a constant presence on set) by not only delivering one of the year's best surprises but Bill Murray's finest performance ever. Set mostly within the confines of the luxurious Park Hyatt Tokyo and in the surrounding sprawl of the Shinjuku and Shibuya districts of the city, *Lost in Translation* is delicate as a cherry blossom in bloom and as gracefully sad as its fleeting beauty. There's a maturity and emotional complexity in the film that is frequently profound, though never calls attention to itself. More understated than *The Virgin Suicides*, which wore its style boldly and without apology, here Coppola drops back a bit, allowing the strange kineticism of Tokyo to overwhelm and to allow her two leads (both superb) to stretch out, improvise, and inhabit their roles in a manner that feels perfect.

But the film's great character *is* the city itself, albeit the city through the eyes of Western tourists. Both stuck in the city for different reasons – Charlotte is accompanying her rock photographer husband John (played by Ribisi, whose vocal inflection and demeanour mimics Sofia's own husband at the time, Spike Jonze) while jet-lagged movie star Bob has been hired to do a series of advertisements shilling a whisky product – the two engage in a friendship that skirts the boundaries of something more, but tactfully and smartly eschews physical intimacy in favour of emotional intensity. This is *Brief Encounter*, David Lean's 1945 classic film about an affair between a young housewife and a married doctor, 'for a more doubting, dyspeptic age'[44] as the reviewer for the *Daily Telegraph* called it. It also stands alongside Linklater's *Before Sunrise* and *Sunset* duo, Gondry's *Eternal Sunshine of the Spotless Mind* and Wong Kar-Wai's *In the Mood for Love* (2000) as one of the finest unordinary romances to come around in many a year.

Like Linklater's films, there's a looseness to Coppola's film that feels vibrant and truthful, whether it's chronicling boredom (shots of Johansson alone in her room, adrift in thought), awkward though hilarious cultural clashes (Murray at the studio filming the adverts) or simply scenes of Johansson losing herself among the tide of people traffic outside of the Shibuya train station or alone in the hush of the temples of Kyoto. This may be tourist Japan, but it is no less real or unfathomable or wonderful.

But wonder is not on the menu for these two characters. They are both desperate, afraid, and lonely. Like much of her father's work, all three of Sofia's films have focused on characters searching for an emotional connection, a way to reaffirm their inner, real selves, removed from family, removed from work, with another person. While Charlotte is still searching, Bob seems almost resigned to his depression and ambivalence toward his family. They are also both privileged – Bob is an international star dissatisfied with his marriage while Charlotte is well educated and has the luxury to not do anything at the moment – though no less alienated because of their wealth or opportunities. Like many of Wes Anderson's characters (and plenty of the fast-talking, affluent protagonists from the screwball comedies of the 1930s and early 1940s), privilege is no barrier to stave off an existential crisis. But as their friendship deepens, their feelings of being imprisoned in a city that neither one of them wanted to be in also begins to change, as when Bob and Charlotte hit the town with friends of hers, proving that it isn't the city per se that enchants but the people who give it life.

Coppola, who spent time in Tokyo in the years following the *Godfather, Part III* debacle designing her own line of clothes, captures the surface of the city with a nonchalant though expressive eye, again courtesy of the magnificent Lance Acord. But she also captures the subtle hush within the electric clamour of the city, the pensive harmony that exists within it too, if the voyager is receptive or open enough to get lost.

While *Lost in Translation* is Coppola's love letter to the city of Tokyo, it's also one to her star Bill Murray. There's no mistaking why Coppola at one point in the film has her two leads sipping sake out of wooden cups while watching Fellini's 1960 masterpiece *La Dolce Vita*, itself a valentine to the city of Rome and to its dashing star Marcello Mastroianni, as well as a perceptive and moving study of alienation amidst the hullabaloo of celebrity. Murray, long a master of the droll, comedic line reading, delivers a nuanced, passive performance that's right up there with the best practitioners of the dynamic reaction – Bogart, De Niro in *Taxi Driver* or *Jackie Brown* (1997), Mastroianni in pretty much anything. It takes skill to pull back in a scene and yet steal it, and Murray has never been better, although his performances in Wes Anderson's films are close behind. Johansson is also exemplary in her role and for a brief moment seemed to be one of the leading actresses of her generation, a volatile mix of intelligence and sexuality and the best voice in film since a young Kathleen Turner… or even Bacall. Although

Johansson had shown great promise in her roles before *Lost in Translation* – as a young runaway in *Manny & Lo* (1996) and as the career-minded, bitchy best friend to Thora Birch in *Ghost World* – it was her role as Charlotte that catapulted her into stardom. Since her breakout role Johansson has given some fine performances – most notably in Woody Allen's 2004 London-based crime thriller *Match Point* – but for the most part her performances have been underwhelming and sadly not lived up to her potential.

Coppola's film was widely heralded as a magnificent, understated achievement, and ended up on several year's best lists. There were dissenters, of course. Most criticism of the film seemed centred on its dramatic restraint and emotional reserve bordering on boredom. But the most vociferous criticism came from the Japanese-American musician Kiku Day, writing for the *Guardian Unlimited*,[45] charging Coppola with racism and cultural imperialism for her portrayal of the modern Japanese as nothing more than stereotypical caricatures, and for depicting 'small, yellow people and their funny ways' while looking back to the country's historical past, its philosophy and artistic culture, with reverence. A similar accusation of racism has often been lobbed at Wes Anderson for his frequent depiction of non-Caucasian ethnic groups as caricatures, though in his case *all* of his characters are exaggerated, with few exceptions.

Despite the low-key controversy, the film racked up plenty of trophies during the awards season. Murray was nominated for a Best Actor Oscar but lost out to Sean Penn for *Mystic River* (2003). He did, though, win the BAFTA for Best Performance by an Actor and a Golden Globe. Johansson, likewise, won a BAFTA for her performance. But it was Coppola's numerous awards, including an Oscar for Best Screenplay, which seemed like the sweetest revenge of all. However, by the time her third film – a longtime dream project about Marie Antoinette – was released three years later, the critics' darling would find a harsher response waiting for her.

Marie Antoinette (2006)

Directed by: Sofia Coppola
Written by: Sofia Coppola
Produced by: Ross Katz, Sofia Coppola
Edited by: Sarah Flack
Cinematography by: Lance Acord
Cast: Kirsten Dunst, Jason Schwartzman, Judy Davis, Rip Torn, Rose Byrne, Asia Argento, Molly Shannon, Shirley Henderson, Danny Huston, Steve Coogan

> 'I wasn't making a political movie about the French Revolution. I was making a portrait of Marie Antoinette and my opinions are in the film.' – Sofia Coppola[46]

> 'When you grow up in France you learn about French history. When you grow up in America, French history is a smaller paragraph in your text book.' – Kirsten Dunst on why she didn't know much about the infamous queen before filming.[47]

It was a subject fit for a member of one of Hollywood's most royal of filmmaking families. Initially inspired to tackle a film about the notorious, eighteenth-century, teenaged Marie Antoinette – who met her demise by guillotine during the peak killing season of the French Revolution at the age of 37 – after listening to her father's longtime friend, production designer Dean Tavoularis, talk about the roundly despised queen's life over dinner,[48] Sofia Coppola no doubt felt a kinship with her subject beyond the historical hype, the gossip, the legend.

And while the film is not the train wreck many expected after word spread of the round of boos from its premiere at the 2006 Cannes Film Festival, nor the vapid, style-over-substance music video many critics have accused it of being, Coppola's wilful desire to take a step back from the political context of the doomed queen (something that it is impossible to do) remains a loaded subject and only highlights Coppola's own insularity within the privileged leisure class that she belongs to. That is not an indictment, merely an observation and an attempt to understand why this promising director – who as a child regularly ran around on her father's film sets, once visited the home of legendary director Akira Kurosawa and could call *Star Wars* creator George Lucas a close family friend[49] – would feel such a connection with one of history's most infamous regal adolescents. It's an understandable commiseration, but no less troubling in regards to the film's ambivalence toward the monarchy's role in one of history's greatest moments of revolutionary apocalypse.

Like all of her films, Coppola frequently has characters waking from sleep, from one dreamland into another. The teenage Maria Antonia, then the 15-year old Archduchess of Austria, is handed over to her French escorts who in turn deliver her to her new husband-to-be, the Dauphin of France, Louis Auguste. Whisked away to Versailles, renamed Marie Antoinette, and surrounded by an elaborate and complicated set of intricate codes, the teenage Dauphine falls away into an intoxicating and bewildering waking dream life that feels at times heartbreakingly poignant as we watch the teenager – still energetic, emotional, and curious – turn jaded, unsure of herself and uncomprehending of her new dollhouse reality.

Dunst, who remains all too vulnerable and human amidst the overwhelming alien splendour of the real Versailles, manages to generate an emotional core to her role, tranquilly exuding a stamina for adaptation while ironically never having the intelligence, strength or inclination to shape her life away from the rituals of the court. As the film progresses from the stages of childlike fascination – the attention paid to the convoluted rituals of even the simplest of tasks such as dressing, eating, waking up – to boredom to outright adult cynicism, Coppola delights in the subtle savagery that becomes a sort of needed armour against the monotony and humourlessness of court life. Asia Argento, another member of true film royalty (her father is the famous Italian horror film director, Dario), plays King Louis XV's mistress Madame du Barry and becomes Marie Antoinette's chief rival in those early days. Coarse, rough around the edges, and defiantly carnal (at least in the film), Madame du Barry is everything that Marie Antoinette is not.

Ultimately, though, there is much cake but little insight. The details are fascinating, but none of it is very sustainable. What understandings concerning the stifling atmosphere that festered at Versailles Coppola does cultivate are nothing new. Stanley Kubrick's own eighteenth-century historical film, the masterful *Barry Lyndon* (1975), plotted out a similarly detached trajectory for his hollow protagonist. But there's a horrifyingly scabrous insight into the emptiness of his main character that Coppola only hints at but is not courageous enough to dissect. In the end, her tragic heroine really is an empty party girl, all flash and no substance – but one Coppola would probably like to hang with nevertheless.

But what wonders are contained in the film are rapturous, lyrical, and melancholic. One of the film's finest moments comes when the young queen is given a retreat house on the grounds so that she can live a carefree – though well-organised – 'emancipated' existence with her daughter. Servants secretly clean the chicken eggs before the little girl holds them, the grounds are manicured ever so professionally, though the queen obliviously lives out her fantasy amongst the manageable idyllic wonderland as if she were roughing it, getting back to nature. It's another layer of make believe and self-delusion, designed to guard her from the realities beyond Versailles that will eventually encroach upon her fantasy world. Yet while living in the artificiality of the countryside, she entertains her friends, engages in recreational drug use, and does her best to remain comfortably numb.

Marie Antoinette is lavishly produced, carefully constructed, and its earnest – though some would say cynical – appeal to the modern hipster youth market, by using anachronistic 1980s New Romantic and post-punk music tracks from Siouxsie & and the Banshees, Gang of Four, Adam & the Ants, the Cure, and Bow Wow Wow, makes for an attractive package. But its director is too comfortable in her hazy complacency, too in love with her subjects to deliver the emotional punch or the cruel incision that an ironist like Kubrick would have made through the gloss. Perhaps Coppola thought history had already taken care of that part.

It was always going to be a difficult third act. As the angry mob (is there any other kind?) marches on Versailles, Coppola seems indifferent to the grim days to come. The energy that crackled in those early scenes has faded and the mindless gaiety has been hijacked by a textbook rabble of extras. Neither the mob nor the audience is rewarded with a sufficient outcome. Coppola, in an attempt to sidetrack history, ends the film with her funky queen and king riding away from their kingdom by carriage, the glow of the morning sunlight holding the splendour of Versailles eternally within their memories, relegating the clamorous mob to run riot off camera along the margins of history instead of in it. The last shot shows the royal bedroom in tatters. But if you didn't know your history, you couldn't be blamed for thinking that the king and queen had simply left for more party provisions, and that everything would be right as rain once the maids tidied up.

MICHEL GONDRY

'When you are a child you are more receptive to the outside world because basically your brain has more space and you capture more detail in everything. But as you grow older you compare all the new information to what you have already, and so the percentage of what comes in becomes less and less. It's the same idea that time seems to pass faster when you grow older.' – Michel Gondry[50]

Like Wes Anderson and Spike Jonze before him, French director Michel Gondry's films crackle with an adolescent's frenetic energy and wiry imagination mixed with a sense of melancholy and emotional defeatism that only comes with age. No wonder Gondry titled his autobiographical short film *I've Been Twelve Forever*. It's precisely at that age that the seemingly endless years of childhood come to an abrupt end, giving way to the tyranny of puberty to mangle and shape-shift one's body into gangly teenagedom. But early adolescence is a transitional stage, and a painful one for those that feel caught between the two realms of childhood and adulthood.

Gondry has directed four feature films and one marvellous concert film (*Dave Chappelle's Block Party*, 2005) so far and is arguably the slightest of the filmmakers discussed in this book, though his second film, *Eternal Sunshine of the Spotless Mind*, is a major exception. It's as close to a real masterpiece as any of the films featured here, displaying both Gondry's technical wizardry and his ability to keep the performances or emotional weight of the film from being bullied into subservience. Not an easy accomplishment by any means. With his supple imagination and perceptive sensitivity toward characters who exhibit a sometimes overwhelming proclivity for their own dreamlife (waking or otherwise), Gondry at times pinwheels across the tinsel and foam night sky like the Cocteau of his generation. There's a fearlessness to his attack upon the rigidity of the banal, an unfashionable, mirthful heroism in the sympathy he obviously has for his downtrodden misfits.

But to label Gondry slight in no way diminishes his keen perception regarding his protagonists' dilemma of being part of the world yet two steps behind it, happily content to observe and drift on the outskirts of drama. Conflict, though, is always near, usually in the form of a girl who the protagonist desires but is too socially reticent to engage, or in the general form of a society suspicious of the outsider and hence willing to mould them into something more manageable and dreadfully respectable.

Gondry himself was raised in the properly bourgeois Versailles, though his family was anything but creatively vacant. His grandfather, Constant Martin, invented the Clavioline in 1947 – a 'monophonic' electronic keyboard that was a forerunner to the synthesiser and used to great effect by everyone from Del Shannon, the Beatles, Joe Meek, John Barry and Ennio Morricone – as well as holding the patents for other musical instruments. His father owned a music shop for many years, and Gondry's own artistic leanings were also never discouraged, whether he was making short films with his brother or banging out music on the drums.

In Gondry's first film, *Human Nature*, his outsiders are literally two wild children (Patricia Arquette plays a woman suffering from a rare genetic disorder causing her body to be covered in fur and Rhys Ifans is Puff, a man/beast who has spent most of his life in the woods far from humanity) who are forced to become 'civilised' once they join human society. As written by Charlie Kaufman, the film (regardless of the faults it's guilty of) symbolically and literally captures the sometimes-painful absurdity of adaptation and assimilation into a new identity. *Eternal Sunshine of the Spotless Mind*, written by Kaufman, Gondry and Pierre Bismuth, explores to great effect the loneliness of doomed lovers – two social 'misfits' who are perpetually destined to find one another yet never destined to be together. And *The Science of Sleep* (2006), Gondry's most autobiographical film to date and the first one based on his own screenplay, focuses on a young graphic designer lost in the head and yearning to fall in love. But what could have easily been a trite, precocious exercise in the celebration of stunted adolescence is given a real poignancy and depth as the film reveals the desperation at the heart of its Peter Pan protagonist, an irresponsible dreamer unable to put down his toys long enough to kiss the girl.

Like the best music video directors, including Spike Jonze, Gondry does not merely shill product or offer up slapdash visuals to lull the viewer into a lotus sleep of pleasing though vapid entertainment. Delicious eye candy it may be, but many of Gondry's best videos – for acts the White Stripes, Björk, Cibo Mato (the video for 'Sugar Water' contains some of the finest use of split-screen cinematography ever), the Chemical Brothers, the Foo Fighters, Beck, his own early pop group Oui Oui (he played drums), and others – display the same sense of melancholy and hyper-realist fantasy that would later be visually explicated in the feature films. As in the video for Björk's 'Human Behaviour', for instance. Gondry also has an uncanny ability to capture many of his most dazzling images via low-tech methods ('Fell in Love with a Girl', 'Dead Leaves and the Dirty Ground' and 'The Hardest Button to Button' for the White Stripes). If Gondry resembles any filmmaker before him, it's the great silent film innovator and special effects trickster, Georges Méliès. Though Walt Disney and Steven Spielberg aren't too far behind either.

In a way, Gondry exemplifies the melding of the avant-garde with the mainstream that so many of this crop of new wave filmmakers seem to have. Wes Anderson, Spike Jonze, even Sofia Coppola to some extent, do not seem bothered in the slightest over notions of 'selling out' or maintaining some quasi-reductionist philosophy about what it means to be an 'independent' filmmaker other than being given the opportunity by the studios to do what they want. Within budgetary limits, of course. All of the filmmakers in this book work within modest budgets for studio films, with the exceptions of David O. Russell with *Three Kings*, Wes Anderson with *The Life Aquatic with Steve Zissou* and Sofia Coppola with *Marie Antoinette*, which were all big-budget films. And in the case of Anderson's and Coppola's offerings, their big-budget efforts were financial flops.

Gondry so far has managed to keep his abundant visual ideas ramshackle and hence low budget, much of the time relying on in-camera solutions instead of CGI and other post-production techniques that would ultimately tarnish the funky low-tech. This mix of lo-fi applications with high-tech concepts, something that he routinely applied for his music video work and advertisements, has helped give his films a look and feel unlike anyone else's. For whatever slightness Gondry's films may have in regards to theme, the textures and emotions in them have been spectacularly memorable and dazzling. And unlike other cinematic fantasists like Terry Gilliam and Tim Burton, creators of sometimes impressive magic themselves, Gondry has never allowed the imagery to become detrimental to the narrative or characters. The creative disharmony that is *Human Nature* was a result of other problems, not because Gondry failed to assimilate his visuals with Kaufman's screenplay.

Human Nature (2001)

Directed by: Michel Gondry
Written by: Charlie Kaufman
Produced by: Anthony Bregman, Ted Hope, Spike Jonze, Charlie Kaufman
Edited by: Russell Icke
Cinematography by: Tim Maurice-Jones
Cast: Patricia Arquette, Rhys Ifans, Tim Robbins, Miranda Otto, Mary Kay Place, Robert Forster, Rosie Perez, Peter Dinklage

'Remember, when in doubt, don't ever do what you really want to do.' – Dr. Bronfman (Tim Robbins) reminding his new living specimen, an 'ape man' named Puff (Rhys Ifans), about the code of Homo sapiens.

In 1996 director Steven Soderbergh came across a script by a then unknown writer by the name of Charlie Kaufman. Unbeknownst to Soderbergh and the rest of the world, Kaufman was set to make a memorable entry with his 1999 film *Being John Malkovich*.

Soderbergh was interested in *Malkovich*, but since the film was already in production with New Line Cinema he opted to purchase the rights to *Human Nature* instead, which he hoped would further the new, stylistically looser and more experimental direction he was heading in (directing *Schizopolis*, featured in this book, and *Gray's Anatomy*, a film version of a Spalding Gray monologue) after a series of critical and financial disappointments.[51] Soderbergh originally wanted TV sitcom actor David Hyde Pierce as Dr. Nathan Bronfman (the role eventually went to Tim Robbins), *Saturday Night Live* comedian Chris Kattan as Puff the 'wild ape man' (a role that went to Welsh actor Rhys Ifans), and Marisa Tomei as Lila, a naturalist cursed with an inordinate amount of body hair and bestselling author of the book *Fuck Humanity*. As bizarre as the film ended up being without Soderbergh's involvement – let alone that cast – the mind does reel.

Told from a variety of flashbacks in a sort of absurdist, cartoon version of *Rashomon* – including from the dead Dr. Bronfman's viewpoint – the film tosses the romantic notion of the 'noble savage' on its head as Bronfman and his wife Lila set out to civilise Puff, a wild man who was abandoned in the woods by his father who thought that his son was an ape. The good doctor, who has devoted his life to weeding the animalistic tendencies out of... animals (one of his experiments focuses on teaching table manners to mice) now devotes his experiments to taming Puff, locking him away within a Plexiglas cage, teaching him etiquette, human speech and the ways *not* to greet a woman in public, as Puff's sex drive is perpetually in overdrive. But Puff isn't the only one with sex on the brain. Everyone in *Human Nature* is motivated by sex and consistently uses it to manipulate others in an attempt to not be alone. Throughout all of Kaufman's work, the fear of loneliness is perhaps the greatest prime motivator of them all.

Unlike Spike Jonze's *Being John Malkovich*, Gondry's first attempt at bringing Kaufman's work to the screen would not be met with the same critical adoration. The story, which is as inexplicably loopy, surreal, and frequently funny as the earlier film, is nevertheless restrained when it should feel dangerous and much too self-satisfied with its own weirdness when it should have the civility to let us figure things out on our own. Gondry's visual sense is as inventive and charged with the same playfulness as in the Björk video *Human Behaviour* he directed, which included a giant teddy bear trouncing through the synthetic toyland woods and a genuine feeling of ecstatic childlike wonder at the menagerie of strangeness unfolding before our eyes. *Human Nature*, in many of the scenes set in the forest, has a similar 'fake' feel to it. Mechanical birds and squirrels inhabit the 'wild' artificial woodland – the whole soundstage forest looking like some psychedelic stereoscopic wonderland – perfectly skewing on a visual level the characters' notions of the noble savagery of man. It's in those scenes where the director and script find a habitable common ground. But when Gondry is forced to settle into the plot and flesh out his characters, many of the scenes fall flat, the performances (Miranda Otto's in particular) frequently tailspin into a strange hysteria even for a film whose tone is that of intentional lunacy and farce.

In the wake of the film's critical drubbing and audience beat down (it made only $705,308 after its brief theatrical run), *Human Nature* has slowly found an appreciative audience who are willing to engage with it on its own feral terms instead of as the stylistic companion piece to *Being John Malkovich*. Although the film as is would've had to fight for respect no matter when it had been released, it was never going to have an easy time as the unfortunate follow-up to a beloved film. But ragged as it may be, with its overload of ideas and Gondry's obvious inability to control the tempo of its scenes and performances (something he would rectify with his next film), there are still many modest pleasures to be found within its hirsute wackiness.

Eternal Sunshine of the Spotless Mind (2004)

Directed by: Michel Gondry
Written by: Charlie Kaufman, Michel Gondry, Pierre Bismuth
Produced by: Anthony Bregman, Steve Golin
Edited by: Valdis Óskarsdóttir
Cinematography by: Ellen Kuras
Cast: Jim Carrey, Kate Winslet, Elijah Wood, Mark Ruffalo, Kirsten Dunst, Tom Wilkinson, Jane Adams, David Cross

'Meet me… in Montauk….'[52] – Clementine (Kate Winslet)

After the disappointment of *Human Nature*, no one would have been surprised if Gondry and Kaufman had never made another film together. But Kaufman's relationships with his directors – the major exception being George Clooney – have always been one of intense collaboration in the truest sense. Kaufman's scripts are not in and of themselves works of art. The screenplay, no matter how well written, no matter how visually evocative it may be, is just a template for the director and crew to shape into… hopefully… something to remember. But the story of their second collaboration would not originate with Kaufman. Gondry and his close friend Pierre Bismuth came up with the film's idea and then brought it to the screenwriter to flesh out. The experience as a whole would turn out to be a much more balanced effort for Gondry than his awkward first attempt with Kaufman.

Eternal Sunshine of the Spotless Mind (its title taken from the Alexander Pope poem *Eloisa to Abelard*), besides being arguably the finest Kaufman film to date, is also an intelligent and gritty rejoinder to the modern variation on the romantic comedy genre, which in recent years has included everything from the sentimental schmaltz fests of *My Big Fat Greek Wedding* (2002) and *Maid in Manhattan* (2002) to the clever, retro-cool Rock Hudson and Doris Day throwback *Down with Love* (2002) and Paul Thomas Anderson's turbulent *Punch-Drunk Love*. While the traditional take on the genre may have seen its last gasp – perhaps for good reason – the genre still seems flexible and durable enough to sustain more adventurous, edgy, and digressive permutations.

As with all of Kaufman's films, the narrative – in this case a story about two lovers, Joel (Jim Carrey) and Clementine (Kate Winslet), who decide to erase each other from one another's memory[53] without telling the other person – is simple. The execution, of course, is a whole other matter. In the pre-credit sequence (lasting 18 minutes) we see a man wake up (to the sound of a van's door being shut?), dress for work and drive to the train station for his morning commute. But while waiting for his train to arrive, the man (seemingly on a whim) runs to an adjacent platform and heads to Montauk instead. He wanders the beach aimlessly and eventually spots a young woman doing much the same thing. While eating at a nearby diner, Joel and the other woman, Clementine, strike up an awkward conversation. Joel is shy, easily bruised and simultaneously attracted and perhaps a bit scared by the erratic girl with the partially blue-dyed hair. On the train back to the city, the two of them meet again, and Joel mostly reacts and sketches in his journal while Clementine does most of the talking. They connect weirdly. Driving home, Joel spots Clementine walking down the sidewalk and offers her a ride. She accepts and the two wind up back at her place for a drink, an invitation for something more, and perhaps the beginning of something. The next night the two of them drive out to an ice lake and spend their time splayed out upon the cracked yet sturdy clean slate looking at the stars. It's a moment that could be extracted from most any romantic comedy, disregarding the fact that our two lovers look like everyday people and that the interiors and city locations look authentically downgrade, lived-in, and funky. Again, just like the places that two single, 30-something misfits would probably live in.

But while Joel waits in the car in front of Clementine's place while she's inside gathering some things for a sleepover at his place, a young man (Elijah Wood) knocks on the driver's side window, startling Joel, and asks him if he needs any help. Joel says no. The young man, looking bewildered himself, asks Joel why he's there. When Joel responds that he doesn't understand what he's saying, the young man flees and we fade to black, only to have the credits roll over a scene (now night) of Joel crying in his car.

Eighteen minutes. And in that time we see a compressed version of a relationship in bloom and then dissolution, an intriguing if slightly confusing prologue to a greater mystery. What we then learn (in reverse) is that Joel has registered with a company called Lacuna Inc., founded and run by the affable Dr. Howard Mierzwiack (Tom Wilkinson) and his small staff in a nondescript building located somewhere in the city, that can erase those 'troubling memories' which hamper a person in their everyday life – bad childhood memories, an embarrassing faux pas, a failed relationship. Joel – and as we later discover, Clementine too – has agreed to the procedure to erase Clementine from his life. But while having the treatment done in his apartment, a part of Joel's mind scrambles to preserve her from cerebral nullification.

While the film has strong fantasy/science fiction undercurrents – it could be viewed as Kaufman's adaptation of a Philip K. Dick book that never was, making up for the fact that his script for an early version of *A Scanner Darkly* was never used – the focus is again on a gritty realism that accentuates the ordinariness of the characters' lives, giving the more fantastical components a verisimilitude that's not distracting or even alarming. Dr. Mierzwiack's urban clinic could well be a dentist's office or a podiatrist's. Nothing is done in secret; nothing looks particularly ominous or unpleasant, which makes the whole process even more unsettling. Though the procedure is a profound experience for the recipient, it's nothing more than a job for the technicians at Lacuna.

In many ways, the film is the antithesis of what passes for cinematic fantasy and science fiction – quiet, emotional and character-driven while still offering up an ingenious plot. But its direct opposition to the modern romance may be its finest coup and deviation. Kaufman's take on the romantic genre is so thoroughly simple yet liberating, you'd think you were watching something revolutionary considering that the modern, mainstream romantic comedy rarely contains characters that are this lonely, paradoxical (they both need one another but also feel smothered by the other person), resigned to disappointment and still open to the possibility for some kind of connection with another person. Clementine, the bookstore employee with the pinwheel eyes and thrift-store witchiness, seems completely approachable and real – though if she were tossed into a film like *You've Got Mail* (1998), Winslet's character would have been relegated to the role of 'eccentric friend' or 'nutty, cute co-worker'. Better yet, she probably would've never made it out of the screenwriter's first draft.

Eternal Sunshine of the Spotless Mind could well be the epitome of the American New Wave: a complex yet commercial film that demands a commitment from the audience but also wants to satisfy, spark an emotional response, and entertain without pandering. Kaufman, like all of the filmmakers of this new wave, wants to provoke us in ways we are perhaps not accustomed to, challenging our conceptions about what an art film can look and feel like, as well as a commercial film. Gondry's direction is completely relaxed here, even though the film's unique visual effects – many of them created in-camera in the Méliès tradition or like a stage production – are even more elaborate than in his previous feature and could have easily dominated the film's delicate atmosphere with the slightest of amplifications.

Unlike Gondry and Kaufman's previous collaboration, *Eternal Sunshine of the Spotless Mind* was immediately hailed as something special, a rare, multi-faceted gem in a desert of Styrofoam rocks. Critic Jonathan Rosenbaum labelled the film a 'masterpiece' and insightfully highlighted a link/reference point to Alain Resnais' 1968 film *Je t'aime, je t'aime*, whose storyline deals with a man who, after attempting suicide, agrees to be sent back in time (initially only for a few minutes) via a pear-shaped time machine. Eventually, the man begins to reshape his troubled relationship with a woman while the lines between the present and past become indistinguishable.[54] Stephanie Zacharek, writing for *Salon*, loved the opening pre-credit sequence and contended that much of the film was 'as daring in [its] emotional directness as anything [she'd] seen in years',[55] but disliked the film's twisty, non-linear narrative as gimmicky and argued that, 'Labyrinthine plots are supposed to stimulate us. But are they really just distracting us from the work at hand – the work of feeling?'[56]

Kaufman has been for the most part publicly quiet since the film's release, his joint win of the Academy Award for Best Original Screenplay and being awarded the distinguished PEN American Center 2005 prize for the screenplay. But while we have had no Kaufman film since 2004, the screenwriter is now donning the proverbial director's hat and embarking on his first feature, *Synecdoche, New York*, which should be out sometime in 2008. No doubt, it will be a film worth waiting for.

The Science of Sleep (2006)

Directed by: Michel Gondry
Written by: Michel Gondry
Produced by: George Bermann
Edited by: Juliette Welfling
Cinematography by: Jean-Louis Bompoint
Cast: Gael García Bernal, Charlotte Gainsbourg, Alain Chabat, Miou-Miou, Pierre Vaneck, Emma de Caunes, Aurélia Petit

Based solely on his own screenplay, Michel Gondry burrowed deep within his own psyche, dreams and obsessions, offering up something almost brutally autobiographical and yet still universal for anyone who has ever spent large portions of their waking life in dream. Stuck somewhere between *The Secret Life of Walter Mitty* (1947) and Terry Gilliam's *Brazil* (1985), the film is a modest comedy that punctuates the familiar clichés of its boy-meets-girl storyline with a series of surreal detours that showcase Gondry's capricious imagination to its fullest. And while the film is no *Eternal Sunshine of the Spotless Mind*, it more than proves that Gondry is capable of carving out his own niche as a prominent filmmaker without the security of a Charlie Kaufman script.

After years living abroad in Mexico, illustrator Stéphane (Bernal) returns home to France at the request of his mother (Miou-Miou), who has found him a job working at a small calendar publisher. Socially awkward and prone to spinning off wildly into his tangential dream world, Stéphane tries to assimilate into office life and keep things interesting by devising projects that are a little closer to his heart and soul, like a calendar of catastrophes. Most of the time, though, Stéphane would rather just host the television chat show in his head, examine the mundane details of his life and pine for the girl literally next door named Stéphanie (Gainsbourg), a shy though self-assured fellow dreamer. At first, Stéphane is more interested in Stéphanie's friend Zoé (de Caunes) than her. But when Zoé doesn't reciprocate his fumbled amorous moves, Stéphane gravitates to her friend, who in some ways is a female doppelganger for Stéphane. Or so he would like to believe. Both of them are vibrantly creative; they like to make toys and gadgets, and are able to unselfconsciously spiral off into childlike fun and games. And of course dreams, which are wondrously visualised using a mix of stop-motion effects, back projection and animation. But there are caution signs about, and despite an attraction to Stéphane, Stéphanie remains hesitant about getting deeply involved with him, though for good reason, as we learn. The film's ending, in which Stéphane inexplicably lashes out at her, is a stunningly honest moment, shattering the illusion we have had of the otherwise likable and inventive weirdo. Gondry, not spellbound by his own creations, pulls back like the mad scientist that he is to display the crippled soul of his child monster. It's an unexpectedly powerful moment, seemingly springing out of nowhere. But the evidence was always there if we stared long enough.

Casually cool and ragged in the best ways, *The Science of Sleep* has the energy of the best kind of lucid dreams and its own internal logic that feels fissured with absurdity and truth. It may lack the transcendence of Gondry's second collaboration with Kaufman, but it shows that the filmmaker has his own personal and mature tales to explore. Critics for the most part were receptive to the film's meandering rambunctious anarchy, extolling the euphoric dream sequences and the performances, but many still found the film slight and perhaps too enamoured of its own whimsy. While lacking the star power and marketing push of *Eternal Sunshine of the Spotless Mind*, audiences were more favourable to the film's hyper-kinetic fantasy and helped the film gross $14,978,490 (twice its budget) worldwide.

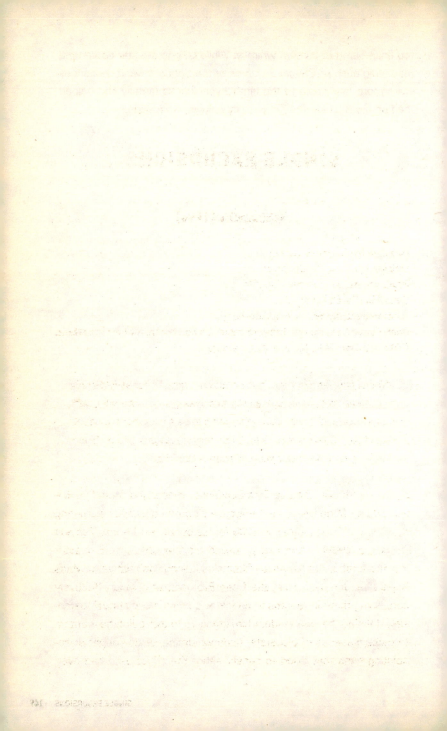

SINGLE EXCURSIONS

Schizopolis (1996)

Directed by: Steven Soderbergh
Written by: Steven Soderbergh
Produced by: John Hardy, John Re
Edited by: Sarah Flack
Cinematography by: Steven Soderbergh
Cast: Steven Soderbergh, Betsy Brantley, David Jensen, Katherine LaNasa, Eddie Jemison, Mike Malone, Ann Hamilton

> 'When I finished *Schizopolis*, I honestly thought… I honestly thought that I was really onto something that was going to be very, very popular. I thought that movie was going to be a hit. I thought people would go, "This is a new thing." I thought it was going to be bigger than *sex, lies and videotape*.' – Steven Soderbergh[57]

By the mid-1990s, the one-time Sundance wunderkind, indie-film darling Steven Soderbergh, had effectively burned out. After garnering the Palme d'Or at Cannes in 1989 for his debut feature *sex, lies and videotape* (1989), a film that propelled the then 26-year-old director into the forefront of American filmmakers alongside relative newbies Spike Lee, Jim Jarmusch, the Coen Brothers, et al (and effectively surpassing them in regards to critical and commercial status), ostensibly defining the independent film ethos up to that point, he went on to make a serious of disparate, underwhelming, or downright disappointing films that failed to satisfy either the critics who had overhyped the young director or the audience who clamoured for more of the same.

Kafka (1991), Soderbergh's dizzyingly black-and-white, deconstructionist mental-monster movie that was less about Magic Prague's finest literary son than it was about the psychic power of German Expressionism's alchemical allure as it foreshadowed the Third Reich's imminent iron march across Europe (see Soderbergh's 2006 revisionist take on the World War II picture, *The Good German*, as a fascinating companion piece), confused and frustrated people with its B-movie-by-way-of-the-arthouse aesthetics. Next came the coming-of-age period drama *King of the Hill* (1993), based on A.E. Hotchner's book of the same name recounting his childhood growing up in St. Louis during the Great Depression, which received good notices and very little else. Soderbergh then directed what would in effect become his creative ground zero – *The Underneath* (1995). Based on the pulp novel by Don Tracy and the 1949 film noir *Criss Cross* starring Burt Lancaster, Yvonne De Carlo, and Dan Duryea at his slimy best, the ill-conceived neo-noir reunited Soderbergh with one of his *sex, lies and videotape* stars, Peter Gallagher, and was stylistically interesting yet ice-pick frigid and brutally sterile. It was an empty mess: distant without being cerebral, and repressed without simmering with the erotic undertow that fuelled the original noirs and many of their simulacra that resurfaced in the post-Tarantino Hollywood that was then just parasitically breaking out. Soderbergh was lost in the cinematic ocean, and it looked as if he might just be drifting away for good.

Structured into three distinct parts, *Schizopolis* is a meandering, fragmented series of improvisational sketches, non-sequitur monologues, daffy Richard Lester by way of Monty Python slapstick visual detours, and moments of insightful, ludicrous parody – all centred on the mental disintegration of one very neurotic, angry, emotionally distant and passive-aggressive American male named Fletcher Munson, dedicatedly played by Soderbergh himself. Munson is also a chronic masturbator which, of course, places him firmly within the pantheon of self-loathing, onanistically minded, Kaufmanesque, solipsistic male protagonists.

The first part focuses on the depressed and suicidal Munson and his inability to function within a stereotypically sterile, white-collar environment (he works for the Eventualism Corporation, a not-so-subtle approximation of the Scientology cult) and his sluggish relationship with his wife, played by his ex-wife Betsy Brantley – a domestic situation so dire, passive, and void of depth that a riot of venom undercutting their banal conversations, their 'generic speak', would be the first step toward a healthy attempt at reconciliation. But Munson is a lost cause, for the most part. Although he is aware enough to know that his workplace and marital situations are completely disastrous for his mental and physical well-being, he lacks the mettle, the grit, or the bollocks to rectify the problems consuming him. And with the imminent arrival of Eventualism's spiritual leader/founder T. Azimuth Schwitters for a gala speech, which Munson has been designated to script after the original speech writer collapsed from a heart attack, Munson's personal apocalypse appears dead on.

The second part of the film primarily centres on Munson's doppelganger, Dr. Korchek (also played by Soderbergh), a jogging, suit-wearing dentist who is carrying on an affair with Munson's wife. While shopping one afternoon, Munson spots his 'shadow self' in a parking lot and follows the mysterious Korchek home. When Munson catches his wife and the corny, joke-telling dentist together, the existential mind-cluster of his situation becomes apparent – he's having an affair with his own wife.

Part three replays much of the film through Mrs. Munson's eyes, reconfiguring the reality of scenes with an entirely new set of rules and different layers of meaning. Whereas in previous scenes Munson and his wife spoke 'generic speak', now Mrs. Munson hears her husband babble in Japanese, delineating how the use of language becomes a barrier when a relationship is on the burn-out. Mrs. Munson eventually leaves Korchek, but any sort of reconciliation with her husband is unlikely.

Initially viewed as a creative lark, a time-out which would enable Soderbergh to rejuvenate his energy, imagination and soul, *Schizopolis* is arguably the most important major artistic move of his career. Filmed with a bare-bones crew of five close friends, with Soderbergh handling duties as cinematographer, the whole affair has the looseness of an elaborate home movie. Which is what it basically is. Outside of a few of the lead actors, most of the cast was comprised of non-actors, family and friends of the director. Set in Baton Rouge, Louisiana, Soderbergh's hometown, the film is audaciously autobiographical in its attempt to peel away the artifice of deception and illusion of a marriage in slow-motion breakdown. At the time of filming, Soderbergh's marriage to Brantley was already over, though, as the director openly stated at the time, the film was in part meant as a way to dissect his own ambivalence about his situation. The film does feel like Soderbergh's cinematic open journal, complete with cryptic passages that are uncomfortable in their specificity and obscure to an outsider. But because the entire work is an absurdist comedy – outrageously broad and unapologetically juvenile – it never feels uncomfortable or psychically bruising.

Schizopolis was barely released theatrically in the US and little seen anywhere else. Critics generally loathed the film, though over the years it has generated a small but dedicated cult of admirers who have picked up on its lunacy, its uninhibited Dadaism by way of sketch-comedy films like *The Groove Tube* (1974), *Tunnel Vision* (1976), and *The Kentucky Fried Movie* (1977), and its perceptive examination of how we cynically use language to obfuscate what we truly want to say. It's a fascinating mess and an amusing trip through the chaos of one man's personal upheaval. Soderbergh has threatened the possibility of a sequel – *Son of Schizopolis* – but so far has not followed through.

But the lessons learned were lessons kept. The years that followed became an artistic boom for the seemingly down-and-out director. Attached to direct both *Being John Malkovich* and *Human Nature* for a time, Soderbergh instead went on to make his true (at least as far as the Hollywood executives were concerned) comeback picture, *Out of Sight* (1998), based on the Elmore Leonard crime novel *Rum Punch* (the second Leonard novel to hit the screens in a year, the other being

Tarantino's *Jackie Brown*). Starring George Clooney and Jennifer Lopez – two actors that sparked with a sexy chemistry reminiscent of the Hollywood match-ups of yore – the film failed to ignite the box office, though critics were pleased to see the newly spry Soderbergh challenging himself once again. In the years that followed, the director would find himself atop the Hollywood dog pile with a succession of critical and financial hits – *Erin Brockovich* and *Traffic* (2000), *Ocean's Eleven* (2001) and its sequels – which peaked with the director being nominated twice (for *Erin Brockovich* and *Traffic*) in the same year by the Academy Awards and BAFTA. He won the Oscar for *Traffic*.

CQ (2001)

Directed by: Roman Coppola
Written by: Roman Coppola
Produced by: Gary Marcus
Edited by: Leslie Jones
Cinematography by: Robert Yeoman
Cast: Jeremy Davies, Angela Lindvall, Elodie Bouchez, Gerard Depardieu, Massimo Ghini, Giancarlo Giannini, John Phillip Law, Jason Schwartzman, Dean Stockwell, Billy Zane

'I just want to capture what's real and honest.'
'And what if it's boring?' – Paul Ballard (Jeremy Davies), a struggling young filmmaker, receives the answer he wasn't looking for from his girlfriend (Elodie Bouchez).

Released in the US in May of 2002 in an altered cut after an unfortunate critical reception at the Cannes International Film Festival in May of 2001 (it went straight to video in the UK and most other European countries if it was released at all), with nary the fanfare or hype that was generated by Sofia Coppola's own debut, Roman Coppola's film not surprisingly failed to draw in much of an audience (its US theatrical gross was $414,358), though its critical reception was more respectable and favourable for the most part. A few critics simply seemed lost, bewildered or simply bored amidst the sea of film references and delicate nods to an era of filmmaking that has been romanticised, for better or worse, by a whole new generation of filmmakers. Critic Dennis Lim, writing for the *Village Voice*, completely understood the historical context that Coppola was paying tribute to, yet called it a film 'of overwhelming waste', 'endearing but pointless', and brutally reinforced the Coppola family nepotism charge that has always followed the clan since the earliest days by lambasting it as 'film dork fantasia... [that] suggests a shopping spree at a high-end vintage emporium underwritten by Daddy's blank check'.[58] The *New York Times* film critic Elvis Mitchell likewise understood the film's pedigree though was more sympathetic to its lightly trippy seductions, noting that 'his [Coppola's] love for the movies, comic books, and music' which suffuse the film 'are basics of pop, informed by a dry, sharp wit to delineate the story'.[59]

The story, simple as it is, focuses on a young American film editor, Paul Ballard (Jeremy Davies), floundering in the post-'68 artistic and political haze and euphoria that was blossoming across much of Western Europe and America at the time. Although ensconced in the European movie biz, Paul is sinking low into a personal and professional malaise, unable to be the boyfriend that his beautiful French girlfriend Marlene (Elodie Bouchez) needs and wants or the happy worker bee that is needed to help bring a tangled, troubled, kitschy, and pretentious B-movie science-fiction 'epic', *Dragonfly*, to completion. Paul simply wants to make his own small, unassuming 16mm film, a personal, black-and-white chronicle of his life in all its mundane detail, but one attempting to capture the real moments. Though as Marlene matter-of-factly says to him at one point, 'And what if it's boring?' In Linklater's *Before Sunrise*, Julie Delpy's character responds in the same way after Ethan Hawke's character explains his idea of filming a man's entire life. It's ironic, since Linklater *is* capable of chronicling the mundane and making it exciting to behold.

In the meantime, the production of *Dragonfly*, which is nearing completion, falls apart when the egomaniacal director Andrezej (Gerard Depardieu) is fired by the film's producer, a larger-than-life Dino De

Laurentiis/Carlo Ponti-type named Enzo (Giancarlo Giannini), during the dailies and Andrezej storms out of the screening room with revolution on the brain. Enzo rashly fires everyone connected with the picture as well, though Paul *is* subsequently rehired to help fix the ending, assisting the new wunderkind director Felix DeMarco (Jason Schwartzman) to patch the whole messy affair up and get it into theatres pronto. The buffoonish DeMarco is a hybrid of Roman Polanski and the late Michael Reeves, a young and promising British horror director who died of a barbiturate overdose in 1969 and who is best known for his shockingly effective and bleak *Witchfinder General* (1968) starring Vincent Price in one of his finest roles (one suspects, though, that neither Polanski nor Reeves were ever as cartoonish as DeMarco). Working with him only fuels Paul's jealousy and passive-aggressive tendencies. When DeMarco is injured in an automobile accident, Paul is promoted to director. But Paul's drifting, sponge-like demeanour soaks up even more turmoil and confusion when he starts to fall for his leading actress, the stunning Valentine (Angela Lindvall). Will Paul be able to finish the film within a few days? Will he be able to keep his relationship ticking with Marlene, or will he hopelessly drift into his infatuation with Valentine? Will he be able to keep his artistic integrity intact? Yes. No. Perhaps. Though maybe he could make up his mind a little sooner if someone would stop sabotaging the production...

Much like Bernardo Bertolucci's love-fest to the same era, *The Dreamers*, *CQ* is more nostalgia and sentiment than an accurate examination of the late 1960s. But it's a celluloid love letter, a modest gem that is like a hot shot of pure pleasure for fans of the period. The major stylistic touchstones in Roman Coppola's film are the heady residue of the *nouvelle vague* and such visually daring commercial products as Mario Bava's *Danger: Diabolik* (1968) and Roger Vadim's *Barbarella: Queen of the Galaxy* (1968). Bava's dazzling hybrid action/ science fiction/spy fantasy is based on the long-running Italian *fumetto* (comic book) about an amoral, supercool, hi-tech thief, Diabolik, and his equally ravishing accomplice Eva Kant, while Vadim's fuzzy-headed swirl of psychedelia pits the naïve yet sexually-aware space-kitten royal, played by Jane Fonda (then married to Vadim), against an assort-ment of killer dolls, a lesbian Queen predator, a venal megalomania-cal scientist, earnest yet dopey revolutionaries, and a vapidly hunky angel named Pygar (played by John Phillip Law, who also starred as the anti-hero Diabolik in Bava's film). Yet *CQ* is no simple parody or pastiche, though it is certainly guilty of nostalgically looking backward to an era of commercial filmmaking that was in the thick of creative experimentalism.

But Bava's and Vadim's *nouvelle* trash opuses are certainly not the only cinema references lovingly sprinkled throughout *CQ*'s short run-ning time. Coppola delicately punctuates the film with visual cues from many of the great European directors of the time, most notably Fellini, Godard, and, of course, Jim McBride's 1967 mock-documentary, ex-perimental feature, *David Holzman's Diary*, starring L.M. Kit Carson. Carson, a low-key yet engaging actor (much like Davies, who gives a stoned, pitch-perfect performance), also co-wrote McBride's *Breathless* remake, Wim Wenders' *Paris, Texas*, Tobe Hooper's follow-up to his seminal American horror classic, *The Texas Chainsaw Massacre* (1974), was a co-producer on Wes Anderson's *Bottle Rocket* (both short film and feature), and has a cameo (blink and you'll miss him) in *CQ* as one of the guardians of conscience inside Paul's mind – namely a critic.

Thankfully, Coppola's homages never feel intrusive or obnoxious. They serve as guideposts, shorthand to the savvy filmgoer, visual or verbal beacons that add to the proceedings – be it a direct visual quote such as Dragonfly sensually rolling around on her spinning white bed covered in cold, hard, American banknotes replete with the face of President Kennedy printed on them, a scene taken from Bava's *Danger: Diabolik*; or more subtle ones such as a Felliniesque camera pan at a party, the sight of Paul dancing on set much like another angst-filled director did on the set of his own science-fiction produc-tion, or a dizzying after-hours ride in a cramped automobile through the narrow backstreets of Rome, a scene that briefly reminds one of Terrence Stamp's nightmarish speed-along in Fellini's masterful short film, *Toby Dammit* (1968). These quotes also help clarify not only Coppola's frames of reference, but those of Paul as well. Like the aesthetically aimless American that he is, Paul's imagination is steeped in the wealth of European cinema that had well invaded the screens of the world by the late 1960s. In the wake of the New Hollywood that was just then making its own sort of revolution happen, Paul will no doubt find his path to making personal pictures, evading any undue creative influence by the suits. With any luck, Paul will stay low to the ground when the bullets start to fly in the fiery aftermath of Michael Cimino's *Heaven's Gate* and Francis Ford Coppola's *One from the Heart* (1982), content to remain obscure, honest, and unsullied by big cash for directing empty studio products, eluding the temptation to become his Toby Dammit doppelganger, who Paul spots during his witching hour sojourn. Then again, considering the fate of director Jim McBride through the 1980s, wherein the once-brazen independent filmmaker made a series of undistinguished, polished, and outright bizarre films such as *Great Balls of Fire* (1989), the Jerry Lee Lewis bio-picture, the sultry New Orleans-based thriller *The Big Easy* (1987), and a strangely fascinating detour of a remake, *Breathless*, starring Richard Gere and Valerie Kaprisky, perhaps Paul should call it a day as a feature film director and avoid the pitfalls to come.

Despite the threadbare script, the film's major strengths are the performances and the exotically hip set designs and kitschy effects, the latter of which are still lovingly exhumed from the past. Roman, who worked on his father's grandiose-yet-vapid horror epic *Bram Stoker's Dracula* (1992) as a second-unit and visual effects director, knows the intricacies of 'in-camera' effects, utilising so-called old-fashioned techniques like forced-perspective model making and other stage trickery, casting the viewer into a refreshingly vibrant pre-CGI illusion, much like Bava remarkably managed to do on the low budgets he was always given.

Roman Coppola, like his sister Sofia, is Hollywood royalty. But neither one has seemed content to simply mimic their father's most successful films – something that would realistically be difficult to do – nor have they been able to coast along on their prestigious family name.

No doubt the Coppola moniker was always going to open doors to these fledgling talents, but if the films had failed artistically (remember Jennifer Lynch's abysmal *Boxing Helena*?), I'm not sure that the studio doors would have been obliged to open up as wide upon their subsequent efforts (at least as far as Sofia is concerned).

Roman, on the other hand, has, as of this writing, *not* followed up *CQ* with another feature film. He seems content to continue working as a second-unit director on a number of films (*Lost in Translation*, *The Life Aquatic with Steve Zissou*, *Marie Antoinette* and his father's latest film, *Youth Without Youth*, released in 2007), numerous music videos for bands such as the Strokes, Green Day, and Phantom Planet, among others, and the occasional television commercial, including spots for Coca-Cola, Nike, Levi's, Gap, and a Burger King ad featuring a fictional, bitchy fashion designer named Ugoff, who, when not referring to himself in the third person, peddles the fast food chain's newest salad line. The advert was a big hit with television and online viewers.

One hopes that Roman Coppola will eventually return to the big screen with another feature film. But the simple fact may be that Roman Coppola, much like the character of Paul, simply has one tale to tell. And that's hardly a sin.

Donnie Darko (2001)

Directed by: Richard Kelly
Written by: Richard Kelly
Produced by: Christopher Ball, Adam Fields, Nancy Juvonen, Sean McKittrick
Edited by: Sam Bauer, Jack Strand
Cinematography by: Steven B. Poster
Cast: Jake Gyllenhaal, Jena Malone, Drew Barrymore, Mary McDonnell, Holmes Osborne, Maggie Gyllenhaal, Katherine Ross, Patrick Swayze, Noah Wyle, Beth Grant, James Duval

'28 days... 6 hours... 42 minutes... 12 seconds. That is when the world... will end.' – The sinister, bunny-suited Cassandra, Frank

(James Duval), stating the inevitable to his new friend, Donnie Darko (Jake Gyllenhaal).

Like a lot of teenagers, Donnie Darko's ride through adolescence is not particularly easygoing – he doesn't get along with his parents, wonderfully played by Mary McDonnell and Holmes Osborne, he hates his sister Elizabeth (Maggie Gyllenhaal) most of the time and hates school even more, even though he is smart and relatively well-liked. Standard teenage angst, for the most part. But Donnie has some problems that are decidedly more intense. Prone to violent rages and sleepwalking, his therapist – played by the always-reliable Katherine Ross – thinks that Donnie is possibly schizophrenic. Donnie *is* mentally unstable, no doubt about that, but the strange currents manipulating him may have nothing to do with mental illness at all. One evening Donnie receives a lesson in how strangely the universe conducts business when he is awoken by an ominous voice and sleepwalks outside to find a menacing-looking stranger, sporting a hideous bunny mask, waiting for him to appear, who calmly warns him that the world will end by the end of the month. The engine of a 747 jet then plummets through the Darko house, directly through Donnie's room, so that it would certainly have killed the young man had he been in bed. The seemingly random occurrence spins the household into confusion, but Donnie spins even deeper as he finds himself at the centre of a series of sinister Fortean wormholes, apocalyptic prophecy, and possible cosmic intelligence known as the 'tangential universe', documented in a book known as *The Philosophy of Time Travel*, which Donnie comes to be in possession of.

From critical hype to audience disappointment to box-office failure to cult zealotry resurrection via DVD to overpraise to complete artistic self-indulgence with the release of a 'Director's Cut', all in the span of three years – the long, strange trip of Richard Kelly's debut film is simultaneously impressive, frantically imaginative, beguiling, informative, and ultimately frustrating. But so is the film itself. It is impossible to predict what fate will befall Kelly's hallucinatory, teenage superhero/science fiction film in the years to come – will it fall away into psychotronic obscurity or will it join the unholy pantheon of true cult classics? One thing *is* clear, though – it was a bona fide, grassroots fan phenomenon when the world needed one the most.

Fresh out of the USC film school, Kelly conceived the story for *Donnie Darko* in white heat visual impressions – an image of a jet engine tumbling toward the subdivisions below and the messianic hero's sacrificial death that would paradoxically prevent the tragedy in the first place – and then fed his highbrow pretensions with plenty of slippages and segues into the territorial pissing grounds of comic-book narrative, the teenage comedies of John Hughes, and the alternate-reality shiftings of writer Philip K. Dick with a little social satire via Vonnegut swirled in for good measure. If it were not for Kelly's strong sense of story and character, though, none of this would have resonated with most critics and viewers as much as it did. Kelly's script, written in five weeks, was not only daring in its convoluted plotting, but in how it tackled science-fiction concepts full on without a reliance on special effects. Except for the crime and horror genres, which can be made on low budgets and gross millions with little marketing and no extravagance (confident style in lieu of effects can go a long way), most independent filmmakers wisely steer clear of science fiction storylines. There are good reasons for this, since a filmmaker with serious intent but limited funds risks damaging their film if it is saddled with Z-grade effects. But films like the indie-favourite *Primer* (2004), which was produced for only $7,000 and went on to win Sundance's Grand Jury prize, and *Donnie Darko* are significant exceptions and lessons in how a filmmaker with an ambitious idea can pull off tricky concepts without blowing the bank. Unlike *Primer*, Kelly's original theatrical version of *Donnie Darko* does contain CGI-generated sequences, but the effects are never particularly elaborate and they are always imperative to the story.

After all the hype, and the blessing bestowed upon it by Sundance Film Festival co-director Geoffrey Gilmore, wherein he rightfully commended Kelly's film for its use of CGI technology and genre preoccupations (something that was both impractical and anathema for many so-called independent filmmakers back in the days before Quentin Tarantino's *Reservoir Dogs* clawed at many of the rigid artistic barriers in 1991), *Donnie Darko* failed to generate much long-lasting buzz at the festival. In fact, Kelly's film had the taint of failure about it and interest from distributors dried up quicker than booze at a writer's convention. Eventually, Newmarket Films picked up the film for $1 million, though they wavered on whether or not it would receive a theatrical release (talk of debuting it on the Starz pay cable network was threatened), something which Kelly believed the deal should be predicated on. Much to the relief of Kelly and everyone directly involved with the film, Newmarket *did* unleash *Donnie Darko* into theatres.

But by the time the film got out there in October of 2001, watching a complicated, surreal, SF hybrid about a time-trippin', manic-depressive teenager, possibly not even in control of his violent impulses, was the last thing an emotionally bruised and bleeding post-9/11 American public could give a shit about. The film bombed. And *Darko*'s 26-year-old director was sure that his blip of a career had as well.

True to the film's twisty take on parallel realities, Kelly's film was resurrected in a manner that hadn't been seen since the heyday of the so-called midnight movie era back in the 1970s, when theatres such as the Elgin and the Waverly routinely showed the raucous and appreciative audiences (their smoke-softened minds alert and primed for the the good, bad, and ugly of film) movies that had been unfairly ignored by the wider public or wilfully discarded by the mainstream critics. Some of the most pivotal cinematic touchstones from that time were George A. Romero's seminal zombie film *Night of the Living Dead* (1968), Alejandro Jodorowsky's mescaline-soaked psychedelic Western *El Topo* (1970), John Waters's classic of filth and more filth, *Pink Flamingos* (1972), Perry Henzell's neglected-all-over-again Jamaican reggae-drenched crime/social realist film *The Harder They Come* (1972), David Lynch's *Eraserhead* (1977), and, of course, the Queen of the bunch, *The Rocky Horror Picture Show* (1975). Not long after *Darko*'s crash-and-burn release, the Pioneer Theatre in Manhattan's East Village began showing Kelly's film at the prime witching hour, turning on a whole new generation to the joys of watching cult films the way they were meant to be viewed – in the dark, with other like-minded freaks, and hopefully under the influence. The film played at the Pioneer for 28 months, and was only pulled when Newmarket decided to release Kelly's 'Director's Cut' into theatres for another go-round in 2004.

The film also generated its fervent cult following on DVD in the US (it was released in May of 2002 and went on to make ten million dollars), and was given a successful UK theatrical release in the fall of 2002, a year after its initial disappointing domestic showing. UK critics and audiences were thankfully far more sympathetic to the delusional Donnie's travails and his relationship with a giant bunny rabbit who warns about the impending end of the world, earning the film a respectable $2 million and also landing Gary Jules's effective and haunting rendition of the Tears for Fears song 'Mad World' at #1 on the UK music charts.

But what is it about *Darko* the film that seeps so deeply inside of viewers? No doubt the film's rubber-room narrative is a major pull, as is Kelly's eagerness to exult in Donnie's emotional downward spiral, imprinting upon the viewer the unapologetic melodrama of stasis at 16. Kelly, with feverish gusto, refuses to distance himself from his tragic hero. Sofia Coppola did much the same thing for her own teenage lament *The Virgin Suicides*, though Kelly's film steers clear of the languid, smeared poeticism for something far more Gothic, surrealistic (more by way of Spielberg than, say, Buñuel) and ultimately more mainstream. Both films trade in adolescent suburban angst and the threat of death and annihilation is ever-present. But Kelly's warped 'superhero' is saddled with the unwieldy yoke of martyrdom, which ultimately forces the twisted adolescent to act beyond his own selfishness and preoccupations. Then again, Donnie may just be crazy. Before the opening credits have even rolled, we are entranced – Donnie wakes up atop a mountainside one morning and cryptically brandishes a smile as he looks down across the valley below, looming above the houses, the shopping malls, the suburban sprawl of affluence and conformity that he calls home. That cryptic smile of Donnie's permeates the proceedings to the very end, lulling us into the film's kitchen-sink plotting, humour, and emotional melancholia with an assured textured style and ambition rare for such a young filmmaker to execute (Kelly was in his mid-20s). It's frequently outstanding, always entertaining and, despite the film's deluge of questions concerning the 'tangential universe', Kelly correctly eases off inundating the viewer with needless explanations about the cosmic mystery afflicting his dark hero. Textured with signs, portents, and subliminal imagery pertaining to Donnie's ultimate fate within the greater mystery, the film rewards viewers willing to step off the plank of reason into the paradoxes that await them.

Much of the film's power would nevertheless be diminished when Kelly released the bloated, over-explicated 'Director's Cut'. Although Kelly has reiterated that the 'Director's Cut' is the way that he would have originally released the film given time and budgetary freedom (music tracks and sound design have been altered, optical effects have been added or accentuated), at 133 minutes (the original theatrical cut runs 113 minutes) it's a plodding affair, stripping the original of its oblique influence and burdening the narrative with needless clarifications (material that had originally been appropriately affixed to the film's website and DVD supplements) about the 'tangential universe' and opting to clarify that Donnie is indeed being manipulated by aliens from another dimension. The film no longer breathes. Instead, it panders to the tyranny of science fiction and fantasy worldbuilding, what writer M. John Harrison branded 'the great clomping foot of nerdism'[60] to describe the incessant need of some writers to rob the reader of doing any exploration on their own. By Kelly needlessly fiddling with his film so soon after its initial release, he has diligently undermined the very attributes – mystery, ambiguity, strangeness – that made viewers fall in love with *Donnie Darko* in the first place.

Five years after the release of his debut, Kelly's long-awaited second feature film *Southland Tales* (2007) premiered at the 2006 Cannes Film Festival. The sprawling, acidic satire of a decadent police-state America in the wake of nuclear warfare, environmental disaster and Earth's ultimate demise within a time and space rip (complete with musical numbers), was not a success with the critics, many of whom felt that Kelly's prodigious imagination and ambition had gotten the best of him. At 160 minutes, the free-flowing apocalyptic fantasy – starring Dwayne 'The Rock' Johnson, Seann William Scott, Sarah Michelle Gellar, Justin Timberlake, Mandy Moore and Kevin Smith – did not fare well. But there were dissenters, most prominently *Village Voice* critic J. Hoberman and Amy Taubin writing for *Film Comment*, both of whom found plenty to admire in Kelly's off-kilter mélange of dystopian nightmare, friendly fascism and cosmic wonder. After Kelly tinkered with the film for over a year, completing many of the special effects, editing the length down and rearranging the structure of the narrative, *Southland Tales* was eventually unleashed upon an unsuspecting public in November 2007.

Punch-Drunk Love (2002)

Directed by: Paul Thomas Anderson
Written by: Paul Thomas Anderson
Produced by: Joanne Sellar, Daniel Lupi, Paul Thomas Anderson
Edited by: Leslie Jones
Cinematography by: Robert Elswit
Cast: Adam Sandler, Emily Watson, Philip Seymour Hoffman, Luis Guzman, Mary Lynn Rajskub

'I'm lookin' at your face and I just wanna smash it. I just wanna fuckin' smash it with a sledgehammer and squeeze it. You're so pretty.'
– Barry Egan (Adam Sandler) professing his heart's desire to his new girlfriend Lena (Emily Watson), the love of his life.

Criticised for years for being self-indulgent, arrogant and, since the release of his dynamic comedic odyssey of the ins-and-outs of the porn industry circa the 1970s, *Boogie Nights* (1997), unable to deliver anything less than epic, Paul Thomas Anderson decided to snap back at his detractors by delivering a short (it runs a brisk 95 minutes), microscopically character-driven love story that refused to shy away from propulsive undercurrents of dread, darkness, and emotional disintegration. In other words, a modern love story. But despite the dark violence flowing deep beneath the film's capriciousness and droll humour, *Punch-Drunk Love* still manages to offer up one of the sweetest and genuinely moving American romantic comedies in decades. It's Anderson's warped, maladjusted masterpiece – bizarrely romantic in its own, unsociable way while gleefully spitting curdled milk in the plastic visage of what passes for romantic comedies. It's a film not afraid to admit that love hurts, and that those it ravages the harshest, perhaps need it more than anything.

Barry Egan (Sandler) is the owner of a lucrative, novelty-toilet-plunger business located in the San Fernando Valley… and an excruciatingly lonely man. Socially maladjusted when it comes to matters of the opposite sex, Barry spends most of his time either working, collecting emotional bruises courtesy of any one of his seven sisters (or sometimes from all of them at once), buying up large amounts of canned pudding in order to win a frequent-flyer sweepstakes, or decompressing at home and calling a sex chat line to actually chat, a naïve act which suddenly turns Barry's life inside out. The next morning, Barry receives a call from the girl he was talking with the previous evening asking for money to help 'pay the rent', and if he doesn't comply she threatens to inform his girlfriend (non-existent) about what a pervert he is. Barry refuses to capitulate, which sets the stage for some possible serious trouble when the sleazy owner of the sex chat line (who also owns a low-rent mattress company), Dean 'Mattress Man' Trumbell (Philip Seymour Hoffman), sends a group of half-wit teenage bruisers his way to settle up. But Barry is invulnerable to the threats, because he is in love – with a mysterious 'piano' that comes into his possession in the most unlikely way one morning, and madly with a woman named Lena who he meets minutes later, seemingly by chance, and slowly learns to surrender to.

Through the course of the film's brisk running time, Anderson sweeps us along on Lena and Barry's emotional Ferris wheel, plunging us into a sometimes-horrifying darkness before raising us up within its rather comforting, old-fashioned romance. That's certainly not to imply that the film is traditional by any means, just that it takes a fabulously perilous detour to the heart. Barry, for all his reserve and childlike gentleness, is also a ticking time bomb of repressed rage. In one of the film's funniest yet most distressing scenes, Barry violently smashes the sliding glass door of one of his sisters, no longer able to withstand their incessant teasing. He unleashes a similar moment of insanity while out to dinner with Lena, destroying the restaurant's bathroom after he finds out that his sister Elizabeth (Mary Lynn Rajskub) has been exposing Lena to embarrassing stories about Barry. But Barry is not the only freak. Underneath her soothing demeanour, self-control and warmth, Lena exudes her own peculiarities – truly strange attractors in a lost orbit.

It is a film awash with dopey radiance, synchronicity, and charged, sublime lyricism, all held together by its committed lead performances – Sandler's brave submission to the passive-aggressiveness of his character is the highlight of his otherwise by-the-numbers comedic career, while Watson, in a role specifically written for her by Anderson, exudes the perfect celestial opacity that has energised all of her work – and Jon Brion's blissfully nuanced score. Brion, who worked on the scores for two of Anderson's previous films, *Hard Eight* aka *Sydney* (1996) and *Magnolia*, as well as *Eternal Sunshine of the Spotless Mind* and *I Heart Huckabees* – all of them stellar in their own right – creates subtle sonic arrangements combined with unsettling harmonies and gigantic sweeping punctuations. Waltzing with hesitation, dislocation and aberrant in a way that claims it as a character in its own right, Brion's score is the aural schizoid colouring of the terror, hesitancy, and rush of romance. It's a score you won't be able to dislodge from your head for days, much like the film. Meshing with the score to accentuate Egan's plummet into true love is the work of digital abstract artist Jeremy Blake,[61] whose floridly radiant colours undulate to the beats, pulsating like a sort of silicone organic hallucination.

While audiences were generally lukewarm in regards to *Punch-Drunk Love*'s seductions and many of Sandler's longtime fans resistant to his stretching out into new territory, critics were more forgiving and many praised the actor's performance. Anderson, like Quentin Tarantino and Wes Anderson, has always had a gift for casting an already established actor and subverting their public or screen persona for his films – Burt Reynolds in *Boogie Nights*; Tom Cruise in *Magnolia*. With Sandler, detecting the turmoil that has always simmered beneath the skin of the comedian, Anderson drew that rage to the surface and captured a performance of a lifetime. It may never wash away the stench of a *Big Daddy* (1999) or *Little Nicky* (2000), but it was an effort worth savouring. Anderson received his own share of accolades, including winning the Best Director award at Cannes, an honour he shared with legendary Korean New Wave director Im Kwon-taek for his film *Chihwaseon* (2002).

Confessions of a Dangerous Mind (2003)

Directed by: George Clooney
Written by: Charlie Kaufman
Produced by: Andrew Lazar
Edited by: Stephen Mirrione
Cinematography by: Newton Thomas Siegel
Cast: Sam Rockwell, Drew Barrymore, George Clooney, Julia Roberts, Rutger Hauer

'There was plastics and television, and I figured television had to be more fun than plastics.' – Chuck Barris[62]

Pop songwriter. Game show producer and creator. CIA assassin. King of trash culture. Author. Salesman. Chuck Barris made his moves upon the world in as many permutations as possible, but in the end, he was still just 'Chuckie Baby' from New Jersey. But in his fictional form, as adapted to the screen by Charlie Kaufman (a script he was commissioned to write in 1997) and actor-turned-director George Clooney, Barris is a man so dissatisfied with his contribution to the world that he vomited that emotion upon the audience he simultaneously loathed and needed for his ratings success. He was lot lice, and fed off the neediness and wish-fulfilment fantasies of the viewers with the appetite of a ravenous cannibal while flinging his self-hate at them with the finesse of a needy child.

After working on popular music television shows like *American Bandstand* in the early 1960s, Barris ended up zooming to the top of the television food chain in the 1960s and 1970s by developing popular game shows such as *The Dating Game*, *The Newlywed Game*, *The $1.98 Beauty Show*, *The New Treasure Hunt* (based on the popular UK show *The Treasure Hunt*, itself based upon a French show), *The Game Game*, and his most notorious and long-lasting contribution to the supposed decline and fall of humanity as we know it... *The Gong Show*. The latter programme, sort of a free-flowing bad trip talent(less) show, complete with ham-fisted cabaret, unfunny jokes, audience participation, and a gaggle of celebrity judges and regular performers including fan favourite Gene Gene the Dancing Machine (an NBC stagehand), Jaye P. Morgan, Arte Johnson, Rip Taylor, and the Unknown Comic (who performed with a brown paper bag covering his head), was a ratings hit for four years. Many critics and moral watchdogs, on the other hand, found the show stupid and a sign of bad times. Stupid it may gleefully have been, but *The Gong Show* now seems like a prophecy of the television world to come – reality shows, 'extreme' game shows, the ever-present chat shows. Looking back at it, *The Gong Show* is still inane. But its blunt-force comedy is no worse than what flickers on the hundreds of television channels now within easy access and it's hardly the harbinger of worse things waiting.

On second thought, maybe it was.

Based on Barris's 'unauthorised autobiography' of the same name, Clooney's film is a kaleidoscopic chronicle of the game show mage's rise as pariah of the nation's airwaves to his supposed shadow life as a CIA assassin, in which he murdered over 30 people around the globe, and his ultimate burn-out. Locked away within a hotel room, a rogue agent, within his own mind like some domestic doppelganger to

Martin Sheen's mentally-blitzed Captain Willard in *Apocalypse Now* (or Howard Hughes in real life), the fallen Barris (Rockwell) thinks back on his life of misrule in the name of fun and tries to rectify his life via his written confessions. Clooney's direction, which lacks a distinctive personality, is nevertheless kinetically visual and always lets his superb cast of actors groove within the super-saturated psychedelic splendour. And does it groove! Drew Barrymore, as Barris's main squeeze Penny, and Rockwell work the charm as best they can, as does Julia Roberts – a fellow assassin and mistress of Barris's – and Clooney as a mustachioed CIA operative/mentor to Barris. All of them are excellent, efficiently making plausible Barris's ludicrous though infectious self-mythologising memoir, but none of them is able to batter through Clooney's obnoxious technical showmanship. There is more than a stain of smugness and self-satisfaction in the air, as well as a rigidity of synthetic theatricality that at times pays off brilliantly – many of the more elaborate scenes were staged and filmed in-camera without CGI or cuts, similar to how Michel Gondry pulled off many of his technical feats in *Eternal Sunshine of the Spotless Mind* – though more often than not smothers with spoof and pastiche. It's an oppressively seedy affair, especially during the film's chronicle of Barris's secret life of knocking off Uncle Sam's enemies – filmed with the paranoid gusto that permeated many of the espionage films of the 1960s and 1970s it appropriates from – but the vibe is as welcome as a prison-yard shank and has the delicacy to match.

What should have been one of Kaufman's best films ended up being merely an interesting and intermittently enjoyable character study with moments of dazzle and little insight. The themes and emotional textures that Kaufman frequently gravitates to – disjunctive personalities, loss of a single identity, a blurring of comedy and existential anguish – are all present. But unlike Kaufman's other collaborations, Clooney did not seek out the writer for a similar meeting of the minds. Instead, despite claiming in numerous interviews that he thought Kaufman's script was one of the best that he had read, Clooney rewrote much of the screenplay without Kaufman's input. While publicising the release of *Eternal Sunshine of the Spotless Mind* in 2004, Kaufman let his feeling be known and lamented Clooney's lack of interest, disavowing the film as 'a movie I don't really relate to'.[63]

This is unfortunate considering Kaufman's own background toiling within the belly of the television machine writing for sitcoms, and also Clooney's experience in the business. The actor, of course, gained success starring as Dr. Doug Ross in television's long-running hospital drama *ER* and his father, Nick Clooney, was a television anchorman and a television game show host in the early 1970s. While the film does not spare the industry from the requisite bludgeoning, it's also a far cry from the howling black moan at the centre of better films, such as Elia Kazan's *A Face in the Crowd* (1957) and Sidney Lumet's *Network* (1976), written by Budd Schulberg and Paddy Chayefsky respectively.

It would be reckless and false to deem it a failure, though. Disappointing though it may be, the film's perfectly realised genius is Rockwell himself. He's the peripatetic centre of the turmoil and delivers one of his finest performances, oscillating with ease between lovable vulnerability and outright despair while mimicking Barris's huckster persona, complete with anxious shuffling, leering reptile grin, and the slippery, carny charm the role demanded.

RESOURCES

DVD

All of the primary films (including many of the music videos directed by Michel Gondry and Spike Jonze) covered in this book are readily available on DVD, sometimes in deluxe editions from specialist companies such as Criterion, and should be easily available from Amazon or any other online DVD retailer, as well as any good independent video rental shop.

Books

The following titles were consulted in the research of this book and are highly recommended for the intrepid neophyte or the well-seasoned veteran cineaste:

Bazin, André, *What is Cinema?* (Volumes 1-2), University of California Press, 1967-1971 (Originally published in France, 1958-1965)

Biskind, Peter, *Down and Dirty Pictures*, Simon & Schuster, 2004

Cagin, Seth & Dray, Philip, *Hollywood Films of the Seventies*, Harper & Row, 1984

Corliss, Richard (ed), *The Hollywood Screenwriters*, Avon, 1972

Hamilton, Ian, *Writers in Hollywood 1915-1951*, Carroll & Graf, 1991

Jacobs, Diane, *Hollywood Renaissance*, Delta, 1980

Milne, Tom (ed), *Godard on Godard*, Da Capo Press, 1986 (Originally published 1972)

Monaco, James, *The New Wave*, Oxford University Press, (1977)

Mottram, James, *The Sundance Kids: How the Mavericks Took Back Hollywood*, Faber and Faber, 2006

Soderbergh, Steven, *Getting Away with It, Or: The Further Adventures of the Luckiest Bastard You Ever Saw – Also Starring Richard Lester as the Man Who Knew More Than He Was Asked*, Faber and Faber, 1999

Thomson, David, *The New Biographical Dictionary of Film*, Knopf, 2004 (Expanded and Updated)

Truffaut, François, *The Films in My Life*, Da Capo Press, 1994 (Originally published in 1978)

Websites

http://www.beingcharliekaufman.com

Fan website hosting all things Charlie Kaufman, including extensive archives of film reviews, interviews, script database, news and a lot more.

http://www.cigarettesandredvines.com

Paul Thomas Anderson fan website.

http://www.rushmore.shootangle.com

Wes Anderson fan website with extensive archives of film reviews, interviews, news and more.

http://www.romancoppolastudio.com

Official Roman Coppola website.

http://www.director-file.com/gondry

Michel Gondry fan site.

http://www.angelfire.com/ca/computersarenotpunk/spikejonze.html

The original Spike Jonze fan website.

http://www.richard-kelly.net/index.php

Richard Kelly fan website.

http://www.detourfilm.com/

Official Richard Linklater website.

http://www.stevensoderbergh.net/

Steven Soderbergh fan website.

NOTES

1   Lim, Dennis, 'Mumblecore: A Generation Finds its Mumble', *New York Times*, August 19 2007.

2   Mottram, James, *The Sundance Kids: How the Mavericks Took Back Hollywood*, Faber and Faber, 2006, p. xv.

3   Lennon, Peter, 'Raoul Coutard: Images of Perfection', *Guardian Unlimited*, June 9 2001, http://film.guardian.co.uk/interview/interviewpages/0,,503948,00.html

4   Sragow, Michael, 'Being Charlie Kaufman', *Salon*, November 11 1999, http://www.salon.com/ent/col/srag/1999/11/11/kaufman/print.html

5   Ulin, David L., 'Why Charlie Kaufman is Us', *Los Angeles Times*, May 16 2006.

6   Kaufman, Anthony, 'Charlie Kaufman: The Man Behind *Malkovich*', http://www.indiewire.com/people/int_Kaufman_Charlie_991027.html

7   Sragow, Michael, 'Being Charlie Kaufman', *Salon*, November 11 1999, http://www.salon.com/ent/col/srag/1999/11/11/kaufman/print.html

8   Proch, Paul & Charlie Kaufman, 'God Bless You, Mr. Vonnegut', *National Lampoon*, October 1983.

9   Johnson, Buzz, 'Jonze and Kaufman Give Columbia a Scare', *FilmStew.com*, October 6 2003, http://www.filmstew.com/ShowArticle.aspx?ContentID=6932

10 Walsh, David, 'An Interview with Director Richard Linklater', *World Socialist Web Site*, March 27 1998, http://www.wsws.org/arts/1998/mar1998/link-m27.shtml

11 Linklater, Richard, *Slacker*, St. Martin's Press, 1992, p.3.

12 Maslin, Janet, 'Mired in the Land of Malls, and Itching for Meaning', *New York Times*, October 11 1996.

13 Ibid

14 Mathews, Jack, 'subUrbia Goes Back to Confused Days', *Los Angeles Times*, February 7 1997.

15 Rosenbaum, Jonathan, 'The Newton Boys', *Chicago Reader*, http://onfilm.chicagoreader.com/movies/capsules/16286_NEWTON_BOYS

16 Linklater, Richard, *Slacker*, DVD, US: Criterion Collection, 2004.

17 Horton, Robert, 'Stranger Than Texas', *Film Comment*, July–August 1990.

18 Feature-length text commentary, *Waking Life*, DVD, US: 20th Century Fox, 2002.

19 http://www.subgenius.com/

20 Mann, Doug, 'Buddhists, Existentialists and Situationists: Waking Up in *Waking Life*', http://publish.uwo.ca/~dmann/waking_essay.htm

21 Smith, Gavin, 'Lost in America', *Film Comment*, July–August 2006.

22 Papamichael, Stella, 'Interview: David O. Russell', *BBC*, November 24 2004, http://www.bbc.co.uk/films/2004/11/24/david_o_russell_i_heart_huckabees_interview.shtml

23 Maslin, Janet, 'Flirting with Disaster', *New York Times*, March 22 1996.

24 Rosenbaum, Jonathan, 'Flirting with Disaster', *Chicago Reader*, http://onfilm.chicagoreader.com/movies/capsules/13421_FLIRTING_WITH_DISASTER

25 Blackwelder, Rob, 'Russell of Arabia', *SPLICEDwire*, September 24 1999, http://www.splicedonline.com/features/russell.html

26 Denby, David, 'Battle States', *New Yorker*, October 4 2004.

27 Sarris, Andrew, 'Guess What, I [Heart] I {Heart} Huckabees, David O. Russell's "Out There" Film', *New York Observer*, October 17 2004.

28 Thomson, David, *The New Biographical Dictionary of Film, Expanded and Updated*, Knopf, 2004, p. 18.

29 McCarthy, Todd, 'The Next Scorsese', *Esquire*, March 2000.

30 Donnelly, Joe, 'The Road Wes Traveled', *LA Weekly*, January 1999.

31 Bennett, Ray, 'The Darjeeling Limited – Bottom Line: A train ride without laughs or charm', *Hollywood Reporter*, September 3 2007, http://www.hollywoodreporter.com/hr/awards_festivals/fest_reviews/article_display.jsp?rid=9718

32 Travers, Peter, 'Fall Movie Preview 2007: The Darjeeling Limited', *Rolling Stone*, September 2007, http://www.rollingstone.com/photos/gallery/16219554/fall_movie_preview_2007/photo/2/large

33 Turan, Kenneth, 'Their Particular Brand of Dysfunction', *Los Angeles Times*, December 14 2001.

34 Rosenbaum, Jonathan, 'The Royal Tenenbaums', *Chicago Reader*, http://onfilm.chicagoreader.com/movies/capsules/21256_ROYAL_TENENBAUMS.html

35 Edelstein, David, 'Capt. Blah. Wes Anderson, the Inert Master of *The Life Aquatic*', *Slate*, December 10 2004, http://www.slate.com/id/2110944/

36 Schickel, Richard, 'A Dive into Divine Comedy', *Time*, January 3 2005.

37 Weiner, Jonah, 'How Wes Anderson Mishandles Race', *Slate*, September 27 2007, http://www.slate.com/id/2174828/pagenum/all/

38 Thomson, David, *The New Biographical Dictionary of Film, Expanded and Updated*, Knopf, 2004, p. 459.

39 Mottram, James, *The Sundance Kids: How the Mavericks Took Back Hollywood*, Faber and Faber, 2006, p. 160.

40 In 2003, a Christian-themed serial-killer novel by Ted Dekker, entitled *Thr3r*, was published. Later, in January of 2007, the film version was released. Both novel and film, which I have not read

or watched, are supposedly similar to Donald Kaufman's fictional serial-killer movie.

41 Wilonsky, Robert, 'Adapt This', *Dallas Observer*, December 19 2002, http://www.dallasobserver.com/2002-12-19/film/adapt-this/full

42 Browne, Caitlin, 'Sofia Coppola: a Fizzy Debut', San Francisco Film Society, 2006.

43 Finke, Nikki, 'Warner's Robinov Bitchslaps Film Women; Gloria All-red Calls for Warner's Boycott', Nikki Finke's Deadline Hollywood Daily, October 5 2007, http://www.deadlinehollywooddaily.com/warners-robinoff-gets-in-catfight-with-girls/

44 'A Brief Encounter for Our Time', *Daily Telegraph*, September 1 2004, http://www.telegraph.co.uk/arts/main.jhtml?xml=/arts/2004/01/09/bflost09.xml

45 Day, Kiku, 'Totally Lost in Translation', *Guardian Unlimited*, January 24 2004, http://www.guardian.co.uk/comment/story/0,,1130137,00.html

46 Waters, Darren, 'Coppola's Period Drama Falls Flat', *BBC News*, May 24 2006, http://news.bbc.co.uk/2/hi/entertainment/5012530.stm

47 Ibid

48 Hirschberg, Lynn, 'So Fia's Paris', *New York Times*, September 24 2006, http://query.nytimes.com/gst/fullpage.html?sec=travel&res=9C07E6DE1031F937A1575AC0A9609C8B63

49 Libby, Brian, 'The Coppola Clan's Best Director?', *Salon*, September 23 2003, http://dir.salon.com/story/ent/movies/int/2003/09/23/sofia_coppola/

50 Clover, Joshua, 'Time's Bullet: the world's dreamiest director lets the eternal sunshine in', *Village Voice*, March 18 2004, http://www.villagevoice.com/film/0412,clover,51998,20.html

51 Soderbergh's early involvement in trying to get *Human Nature* off the ground is detailed in the book *Getting Away with It, Or: The Further Adventures of the Luckiest Bastard You Ever Saw – Also Starring Richard Lester as the Man Who Knew More Than He Was Asked*, Faber and Faber, 1999.

52 Besides being the farthest into the Atlantic New York stretches, and a renowned fishing area, Montauk, Long Island, is also home to one of the strangest conspiracy theories around. Known as the Montauk Project, and dealt with in minute detail in a series of books by authors Preston B. Nichols and Peter Moon, the area in the years following WW II supposedly became a base for a group of rogue US military scientists to conduct a series of mind-control experiments. The experiments, as recalled by Nichols, who claimed to be an 'unwitting victim' of the tests, eventually ripped through the fabric of space and time, forever altering our world and thrusting us into a cosmic time shift we've been un-able to extract ourselves from despite the 'fact' the tests ended in 1983. Whether or not this bizarre slice of crypto-paranoiac lore influenced Charlie Kaufman to set part of his story there is… un-known.

53 In July 2007, a report published in the *Journal of Psychiatric Research* stated that the drug propranolol combined with therapy could reduce unwanted memories in patients suffering from trauma.

54 Rosenbaum, Jonathan, 'A Stylist Hits His Stride', *Chicago Reader*, March 04 2004, http://www.chicagoreader.com/movies/archives/2004/0304/040319.html

55 Zacharek, Stephanie, 'Brilliant Mistake', *Salon*, March 19 2004, http://dir.salon.com/story/ent/movies/review/2004/03/19/eternal_sunshine/index2.html

56 Ibid

57 Indresek, Scott, 'Interview with Steven Soderbergh', *The Believer*, August 2006.

58 Lim, Dennis, 'Le Chic by Geek', *Village Voice*, May 22–28 2002, http://www.villagevoice.com/film/0221,lim,34972,20.html

59 Mitchell, Elvis, '*CQ*', *New York Times*, May 24 2002.

60 Harrison, M. John, 'very afraid', *Uncle Zip's Window*, January 27 2007, http://uzwi.wordpress.com/2007/01/27/very-afraid/

61 On July 17 2007, the 35-year-old Blake, considered to be a pioneer in digital 'moving paintings', committed suicide by swimming out

to sea off of New York's Rockaway Beach. Five days later his body washed ashore. A suicide note was found simply stating that he could not live without his longtime girlfriend Theresa Duncan, a computer game designer, who had committed suicide on July 10 2007.

62 Rabin, Nathan, 'Interviews: Chuck Barris', *The A.V. Club*, May 28 2003, http://www.avclub.com/content/node/22525

63 Smith, Neil, 'Inside Screenwriter Kaufman's Mind', *BBC News Online*, April 28 2004, http://news.bbc.co.uk/1/hi/entertainment/film/3664683.stm

INDEX